Good Cooking Habits

for
Fran —
eat —
drink
and
enjoy —

Your sister —
Karen

Karol Jackowski's life as a nun began in 1964 when she joined the Sisters of the Holy Cross in South Bend, Indiana. She graduated from Saint Mary's College in South Bend in 1969 with a B.A. in sociology, and then from the University of Notre Dame in 1974 with a M.A. in theology.

Karol spent half of her life as a nun at Saint Mary's College, first as a student and then as an administrator in various capacities. In 1990, she moved to New York City to finish her Ph.D. at New York University. During this time, she also was the chief operating officer of an East Village novelty store called Alphabets.

In 1995, Karol left the Sisters of the Holy Cross and became part of the Sisters for Christian Community, an independent, self-governing sisterhood. Karol is now a full-time writer and is also the author of *Sister Karol's Book of Spells and Blessings, Ten Fun Things To Do Before You Die*, and *The Silence We Keep*. She lives in New York City.

food for

your body

your soul

and

your funnybone

Good Cooking Habits

by nun other than *Sr. Karol Jackowski*

Forest of Peace ⬥ Notre Dame, IN

Quotes from the Constitution are from the Constitution of the Congregation of the Sisters of the Holy Cross, 1962.

www.forestofpeace.com

International Standard Book Number: 0-939516-73-X

Cover and text design by John Carson

Photos: pg. 5 © gettyimages; pgs. 9, 32, 76, 98 © Corbis; pg. 56 © Alamy Ltd. All rights reserved.

Printed and bound in the United States of America.

Library of Congress Cataloging-in-Publication Data
Jackowski, Karol.
  Good cooking habits : food for your soul, your stomach, and your funnybone / from nun [sic] other than Sister Karol Jackowski.
      p. cm.
  Includes index.
  ISBN 0-939516-73-X (pbk.)
  1. Cookery, American. 2. Jackowski, Karol--Humor. I. Title.
  TX715.J125 2005
  641.5973--dc22
                                 2005010164

Contents

Introduction

Twenty-five years ago, Ave Maria Press published *Let the Good Times Roll* and *Home on the Range*, two cookbooks written for the college students I was living with at the time. I was a Residence Hall Director at Saint Mary's College then and the only way I could get students to attend a meeting was to feed them. The cookbooks contained the most successful recipes, and were first run off on orange and yellow paper and given to the Resident Assistants for Christmas presents. I hand-printed the recipes; illustrated them with drawings, quotes, jokes, and fascinating facts; and even designed the front cover and made up what the critics had to say on the back. Frank Cunningham at Ave Maria Press is the one who found them, published them, and turned them into something far beyond my wildest imaginings. That was the beginning of my life as a writer and I owe it all to Frank Cunningham.

This book I also owe to Frank. It was his idea that we resurrect the best of **Let the Good Times Roll** and **Home on the Range**, and add some recipes of the best food I've eaten in the past twenty-five years. We've also added some new quotes and fascinating facts, some of the funniest stories from my life as a nun, and some photos of nuns doing funny things.

The image of the habited nun doing funny things is, oddly enough, still the popular image that comes to mind when we hear the word "nun." It's odd in reference to me because I was that kind of nun for only five years, and the kind of nun I am now could not be farther removed from that image. The kind of nun most of us are now is so ordinary in manner and appearance, that there is no image to replace the habited archetype we still revere. This book celebrates everything I was and everything I am today as a sister, the extraordinary and the ordinary, the heart and soul of sisterhood that remains when the habit is removed, with all of its exclusiveness, and the manner of religious life becomes ordinary.

The one thing that has never changed in the sisterhood is how holy meals are and how sacred the time is that we spend around the table. I am a member of the Sisters for Christian Community now, and whenever we get together for our monthly meetings, we spend hours around the table filling in the blanks of our lives since we last met, sharing thoughts and prayers, and laughing until we cry over stories from our lives in the sisterhood. While we come from different religious communities, the experiences are remarkably the same, and just as funny. What happens around the table when we come together is Eucharist, pure and simple. Our love for one another blesses the food that we share and it never fails that I always leave them feeling full of a kind of "soul food" found only in sisterhood, found only when friends and loved ones sit around the table and share how sacred our lives are, and how much fun even the worst of times can be.

It is my hope that this book of recipes provides you with everything you need to turn every meal into Eucharist for your family and friends. It is my hope that when you gather around the table with those you love, you too find your souls fed by so much laughter and fun that you taste and see for yourself the pure joy I find in sisterhood.

In the sacred space of our homes, every dining room table is an altar and every meal is Eucharist for those who love one another. Blessings on you and all those gathered around your table.

Karol in kindergarten, 1951.

Spirited Drinks and Appetizers

Superiors shall combat in their houses whatever may savor of sensuality, in order to forestall even the slightest abuse. Beverages with alcoholic content shall not be used except on special occasions and with extreme moderation. No sister may have such beverages at her disposal without explicit permission of her superiors.
—Constitution #222

As a young nun in 1964, part of my Sunday schedule was visiting the elderly sisters in the convent infirmary. I was given the name of Sister Concilio to visit; a high-spirited old nun who lived across the hall from her best friend, Sister Evangelista, another live-wire. They were known as "Concil" and "Vange," and had a reputation for loving the young sisters. They called us "kids." After each of the first three open-door visits I left with a pocket full of hard candy. On the fourth visit the door was closed and I left with something far more precious.

"Kid," Sister Concil said, "Can you keep a secret?"

When I said, "Of course," Concil got up from her rocking chair, closed the door, turned the lock, and gave me a fiendish grin I can still see today. She opened the closet, reached behind some boxes, and pulled out a pink crocheted poodle, the kind designed to cover a bottle. She held it like a baby.

"Would you like a little C.C. from my baby?" she whispered, grinning.

To make a wonderful seven year story short, not only did we share a little Canadian Club that day and nearly every visiting day thereafter, but I became one of many sisterly accomplices that kept the poodle alive. I drove Concil to doctor's appointments and on the way home stopped, at her insistence, at the liquor store, where she dumped about two dollars in change on the counter, smiled sheepishly, and asked in a sweet old nun way for a fifth of C.C. She got it every time without question and with an even bigger smile from the guy behind the counter. Every time I rolled my eyes in disbelief and was responsible for disposing the empties and sneaking in the refills. Those deep habit pockets covered a

multitude of sins. After seven years of what she called "holy disobedience," Concil's health began to fail and our conversations turned more and more to her days being numbered.

"Kid," she said, "When I go, get the poodle. Don't let anyone find the poodle."

Why she cared about the poodle after she died was beyond me, but she did. She put my hand on the Bible, wrapped her rosary around my fingers, and made me swear I would get the poodle when she died. The last time I saw Concil was three days before she died. Her parting words, nearly breathless, were "get . . . the . . . poodle. . . ."

I did get the poodle when Sister Concilio died, and was also given her rosary which I still pray every night with Concil in mind. I don't remember what happened to the crocheted poodle after the C.C. was gone, but I do remember that several sisters had such beverages at their disposal without the permission of the superior and no one seemed to mind. Concil wasn't the only infirmed sister with a poodle, and somehow that exception to the holy rule was silently permitted. One of the finest features of the sisterhood is still its enjoyment of distilled spirits, with moderation of course, but not *extreme* moderation. We are believers of moderation in all things, including moderation.

Sister Concil

Spirited Drinks

GOOD NIGHT EGGNOG

Serves 8

6 large egg yolks

1 cup powdered sugar

2 cups rum, brandy, or bourbon

1 cup heavy cream

1 1/4 cup whole milk

6 egg whites

pinch of salt

nutmeg (fresh)

1. Put egg yolks and 3/4 cup sugar in a bowl and whisk until mixture thickens and egg yolks lighten. Continue whisking and drizzle in 1 cup of rum or bourbon. The texture should be thick and creamy. Cover and refrigerate for 1 hour.

2. With an electric mixer, blend remaining liquor into refrigerated mixture, then add heavy cream and milk. More milk can be added if it's too thick.

3. In a separate bowl, whisk egg whites until fluffy, adding a pinch of salt. Add the rest of the sugar slowly and keep whisking until well blended. The egg whites should hold their own, but not be stiff peaks. Then with a wooden spoon gently fold the egg whites into the egg mixture, blending well.

4. Grate fresh nutmeg on top and serve.

> Good night, and sweet dreams.

GOOD MORNING
BLOODY MARYS

Serves 6

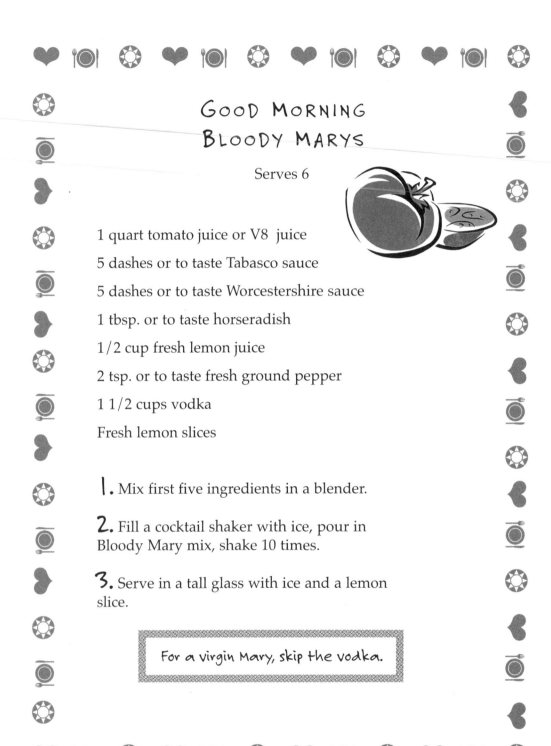

1 quart tomato juice or V8 juice

5 dashes or to taste Tabasco sauce

5 dashes or to taste Worcestershire sauce

1 tbsp. or to taste horseradish

1/2 cup fresh lemon juice

2 tsp. or to taste fresh ground pepper

1 1/2 cups vodka

Fresh lemon slices

1. Mix first five ingredients in a blender.

2. Fill a cocktail shaker with ice, pour in Bloody Mary mix, shake 10 times.

3. Serve in a tall glass with ice and a lemon slice.

> For a virgin Mary, skip the vodka.

Best of the Bellinis

PEACH BELLINIS

2 oz. peach nectar, chilled
4 oz. champagne, chilled
Fresh raspberries

In a champagne flute, add peach nectar and champagne. Stir gently and garnish with fresh raspberries.

APRICOT BELLINIS

6 fresh apricots, halved; or 1-17 oz. can of apricot halves, drained.
1-11 oz. can of apricot nectar, chilled
1 1/2 cups champagne, chilled
fresh apricot slices
crushed ice

In a blender, process the apricots and nectar until smooth. Stir in champagne, pour over crushed ice, and garnish with a fresh apricot slice.

Margaritaville

TRADITIONAL SALLY DAVIES MARGARITA

1 part tequila

2 parts triple sec

1/2 fresh lime (never, ever use bottled lime juice)

lots of ice

1. Fill tall glass with ice.

2. Pour in tequila, triple sec, and juice of 1/2 fresh lime.

3. Cover glass tightly with plastic wrap and shake 20 times. Serve with ice, or straight up with a slice of fresh lime.

POMEGRANATE MARGARITA

1 part tequila

2 parts triple sec

1/2 fresh lime

pomegranate juice

lots of ice

1. Fill tall glass with ice.

2. Pour in tequila, triple sec, fresh lime juice, then fill rest of glass with pomegranate juice.

3. Cover glass tightly with plastic wrap and shake 20 times. Serve straight up or over ice with a slice of fresh lime.

BLOOD ORANGE MARGARITA

1 part tequila

2 parts triple sec

1/2 fresh lime

blood orange juice

blood orange slices

lots of ice

1. Fill tall glass with ice.

2. Pour in tequila, triple sec, fresh lime juice, then fill rest of glass with blood orange juice.

3. Cover glass tightly with plastic wrap and shake 20 times. Serve straight up or over ice with a slice of blood orange.

MY COSMOPOLITANS

1 part vodka
2 parts triple sec
1/2 fresh lime (never, ever use bottled lime juice)
cranberry juice
lots of ice

1. Fill tall glass with ice.

2. Pour in vodka, triple sec, juice of 1/2 lime, then fill rest of glass with cranberry juice.

3. Cover glass tightly with plastic wrap and shake 20 times. Serve straight up or over ice with a slice of fresh lime.

JUDY'S MANHATTANS

3 parts whiskey
1 part sweet vermouth
maraschino cherries
ice

Pour whiskey and sweet vermouth over ice, adding a drop or two of maraschino cherry juice. Stir and serve straight up in a martini glass, or on the rocks. Garnish with one or two maraschino cherries.

Spirited Appetizers

Hot Artichoke Dip

1-8 oz. can artichoke hearts, drained and coarsely chopped
1 cup mayonnaise
1 cup fresh grated Parmesan cheese
Greek olives (optional)
crackers

1. Mix hearts, mayonnaise, and Parmesan cheese in a baking dish.

2. If you like Greek olives, scatter some on top.

3. Bake at 350° for 30 minutes, or until it starts to brown and bubble.

> Serve with crisp, sturdy, salted crackers.

Simply Divine
Vegetable Dip

1-8 oz. container of sour cream

1 packet powdered Italian dressing mix

fresh vegetables for dipping (carrots, celery, red and green pepper strips, broccoli, cauliflower, etc.)

1. Add dressing mix to sour cream and blend well.

2. Let sit overnight for flavors to blend.

3. Serve with fresh veggies.

LONNIE THE LANDSCAPER'S GUACAMOLE

4 ripe avocados, coarsely mashed
2 tbsp. fresh lime juice
1 Vidalia onion, finely chopped
2 garlic cloves, minced
4 plum tomatoes, seeded and finely chopped
3 tbsp. fresh cilantro, chopped
2 fresh jalapeños, seeded and minced
salt to taste
tortilla chips

1. Mix avocados with lime juice and set aside.

2. Mix other ingredients well and blend with avocado.

3. Serve with tortilla chips.

Lonnie Zamora was a landscaper for Martha Stewart. I met him at a party in New York City and he brought the guacamole. I got the recipe and never saw him again.

MINI MEXICAN PIZZAS
(NACHITOS)

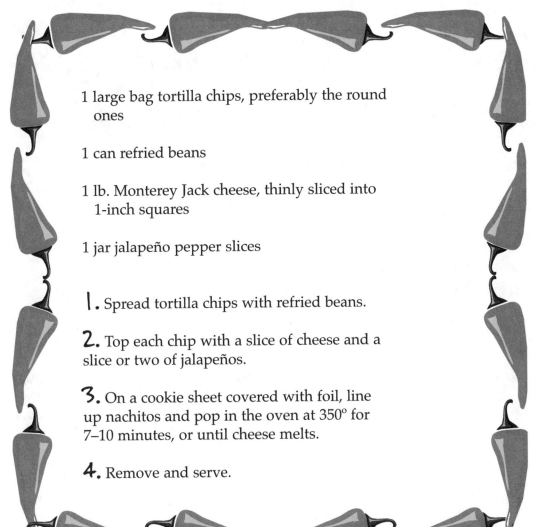

1 large bag tortilla chips, preferably the round ones

1 can refried beans

1 lb. Monterey Jack cheese, thinly sliced into 1-inch squares

1 jar jalapeño pepper slices

1. Spread tortilla chips with refried beans.

2. Top each chip with a slice of cheese and a slice or two of jalapeños.

3. On a cookie sheet covered with foil, line up nachitos and pop in the oven at 350° for 7–10 minutes, or until cheese melts.

4. Remove and serve.

Figure on 4 to 6 nachitos per person.
O Dios mío, these are good!

PARMESAN CHEESE BREAD

1 large baguette or French bread
1/3 cup olive oil
1 tsp. finely minced garlic
1 1/2 cup freshly grated Parmesan cheese

1. Add garlic to oil and mix. Let sit for 2 hours.

2. Split loaf of bread in half lengthwise.

3. Brush garlic oil over bread and sprinkle with cheese.

4. Bake for 10 minutes at 450°. Remove and cut into bite-size servings.

BRUSCHETTA

3 cups ripe plum tomatoes, peeled, seeded, and
　　diced

5 tbsp. fresh basil leaves, chopped

1 tbsp. garlic, minced

1/4 cup extra virgin olive oil

salt and freshly ground pepper, to taste

1 loaf Italian bread

1. Combine the first five ingredients and let them
marinate at room temperature for at least 1 hour.

2. Cut the loaf of Italian bread into 1/2-inch slices
and toast them.

3. When ready, spoon the tomato mixture onto the
toasted bread and serve.

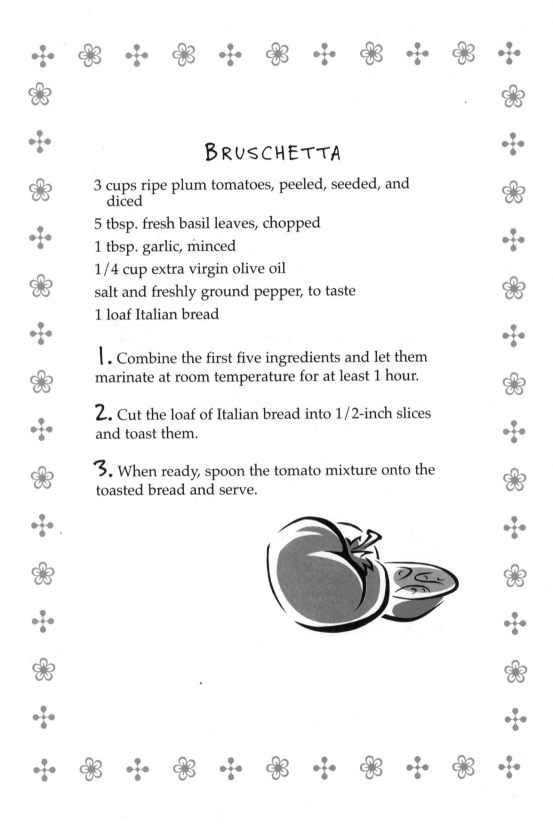

BAKED STUFFED MUSHROOMS

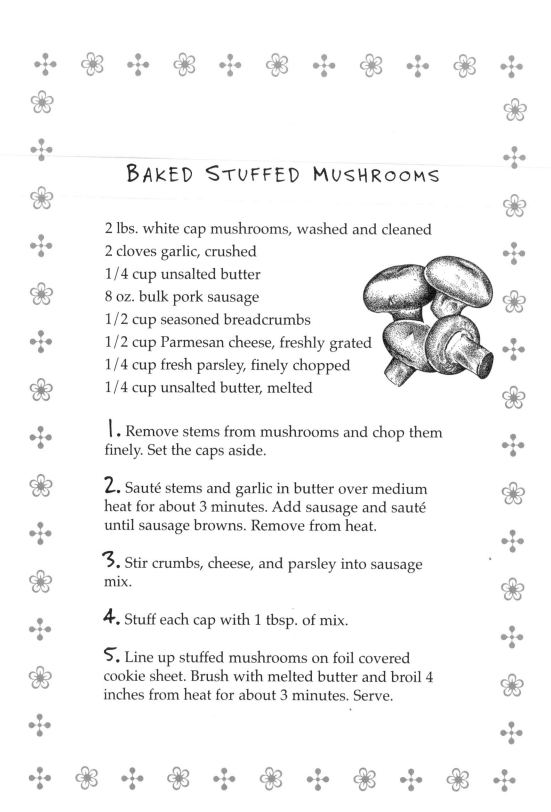

2 lbs. white cap mushrooms, washed and cleaned
2 cloves garlic, crushed
1/4 cup unsalted butter
8 oz. bulk pork sausage
1/2 cup seasoned breadcrumbs
1/2 cup Parmesan cheese, freshly grated
1/4 cup fresh parsley, finely chopped
1/4 cup unsalted butter, melted

1. Remove stems from mushrooms and chop them finely. Set the caps aside.

2. Sauté stems and garlic in butter over medium heat for about 3 minutes. Add sausage and sauté until sausage browns. Remove from heat.

3. Stir crumbs, cheese, and parsley into sausage mix.

4. Stuff each cap with 1 tbsp. of mix.

5. Line up stuffed mushrooms on foil covered cookie sheet. Brush with melted butter and broil 4 inches from heat for about 3 minutes. Serve.

CHICKEN FINGERS WITH HONEY MUSTARD

Serves 6

4 skinless and boneless chicken breasts
1 cup milk
1 cup all-purpose flour
1 tsp. salt
1/2 tsp. freshly ground pepper
1/4 tsp. cayenne pepper
1 cup vegetable oil, for frying

Honey Mustard
1/2 cup honey
1/4 cup Dijon mustard

1. In a small bowl, mix ingredients for honey mustard 2 days in advance. Flavors need time to blend.

2. Cut chicken breasts into dipping-size strips.

3. Pour milk in a shallow bowl. Mix flour and seasonings in another bowl.

4. Dip chicken in milk, then coat well with flour mixture.

5. Pour 1/4 inch of oil in large skillet. Heat on medium high heat until hot enough for frying.

6. Set chicken strips in hot oil and fry about 3 minutes on each side, turning only once. The more you turn it, the tougher the chicken gets. Strips should be golden brown and crisp.

7. Drain on paper towel and serve with sauce.

> Finger lickin' good.

25

Buffalo Wings with Blue Cheese Dip

Wings

12 chicken wings, cut up (remove tips)
1/4 cup salted butter, melted
1 tbsp. hot red pepper sauce
1/4 tsp. cayenne pepper
1 tbsp. soy sauce

1/3 cup brown sugar
3 garlic cloves, minced
carrot and celery sticks

1. Mix butter, hot sauce, pepper, soy sauce, sugar, and garlic well.

2. Dip chicken parts in sauce and place on foil covered baking sheet.

3. Bake at 400° for 45 minutes, basting frequently with sauce.

4. Just before serving, pour rest of sauce over wings and broil for 1 minute to crisp skin. Serve with carrot and celery sticks and blue cheese dip.

Blue Cheese Dip

1-8 oz. package cream cheese
1/2 cup sour cream
1/3 cup mayonnaise
2 tsp. Worcestershire sauce
1/2 tsp. white pepper
salt to taste
1 cup crumbled blue cheese

1. Mix first six ingredients in food processor until smooth and creamy.

2. Add crumbled blue cheese and mix in by hand.

3. Refrigerate until ready to use.

Sister Deb's Bacon and Water Chestnuts

Makes about 24

1 lb. bacon
2 cans water chestnuts, drained
1 1/2 cups ketchup
3/4 cup white sugar
1/4 cup brown sugar
toothpicks

1. Cut bacon slices into thirds.

2. Take the cut bacon, wrap around a water chestnut, and secure with a toothpick.

3. Bake on foil lined cookie sheet at 350° for 15 minutes. Drain off fat.

4. Mix ketchup and sugars well, pour over water chestnuts, and bake 15 minutes more at 350°.

> This "Sister" Deb is not a nun. She's my younger sister. I also have a Sister Jackie.

27

BRENDA'S SWEET AND SOUR MEATBALLS

Meatballs

1 lb. lean ground beef	1 tsp. garlic salt
1/4 cup bread crumbs	1/2 tsp. black pepper
1/3 cup onion, diced extremely fine	vegetable oil

1. Combine all ingredients (except oil) in a bowl, but don't over mix.

2. Use enough of the meat mixture to make a 3/4-inch meatball. Place the meat in your hand and squeeze only two times, rolling into ball.

3. Put meatballs in heavy skillet and add a little oil to prevent sticking. Brown over medium heat, then remove from pan.

Sauce

1/3 cup sugar	1/3 cup water
1/3 cup white vinegar	2 tbsp. cornstarch
1/3 cup soy sauce	
1 chicken bouillon cube	

1. Using the same skillet, combine everything except cornstarch and bring to a boil. Make sure the bouillon cube dissolves.

2. In a small dish, add cornstarch and a few drops of water to make a runny paste.

3. Add cornstarch paste slowly to skillet, just enough to thicken sauce. Discard the rest.

4. Add meatballs to the sauce, bring to a boil, and serve over rice or as an appetizer.

CHICKEN SATAY WITH PEANUT SAUCE

Makes about 50 pieces

Chicken

1 1/2 lbs. boneless, skinless
   chicken breasts
3 tbsp. corn oil
3 tbsp. sesame oil
1/3 cup dry sherry
1/3 cup soy sauce

3 tbsp. lemon juice
2 tsp. minced garlic
2 tsp. minced ginger
1/4 tsp. fresh ground pepper
3 dashes Tabasco sauce

1. Cut chicken into strips 1/2-inch wide and 3 inches long.

2. Mix remaining ingredients well, add chicken, and marinate
in the refrigerator anywhere from 4 to 12 hours.

Sauce

2 tsp. sesame oil
4 tsp. corn oil
2 tbsp. minced garlic
1 tsp. minced ginger
1/2 cup minced red onion
1 tbsp. red wine vinegar
1 1/2 tbsp. brown sugar

1/3 cup chunky peanut butter
3 tbsp. ketchup
3 tbsp. soy sauce
1 tbsp. fresh lime juice
2 dashes Tabasco sauce
1/3 cup hot water

1. In small saucepan heat sesame and corn oils. Add garlic,
ginger, and onion and sauté until soft. Add vinegar and sugar,
stirring until sugar dissolves.

2. Remove from heat, and stir in rest of ingredients. Can also
blend in food processor.

3. Season to taste. Cool to room temperature.

4. Preheat over to 375°.

5. Thread chicken on skewers or toothpicks and bake on a
cookie sheet for 8–10 minutes.

6. Serve hot with sauce.

Well worth the time
and effort.

29

SHRIMP COCKTAIL

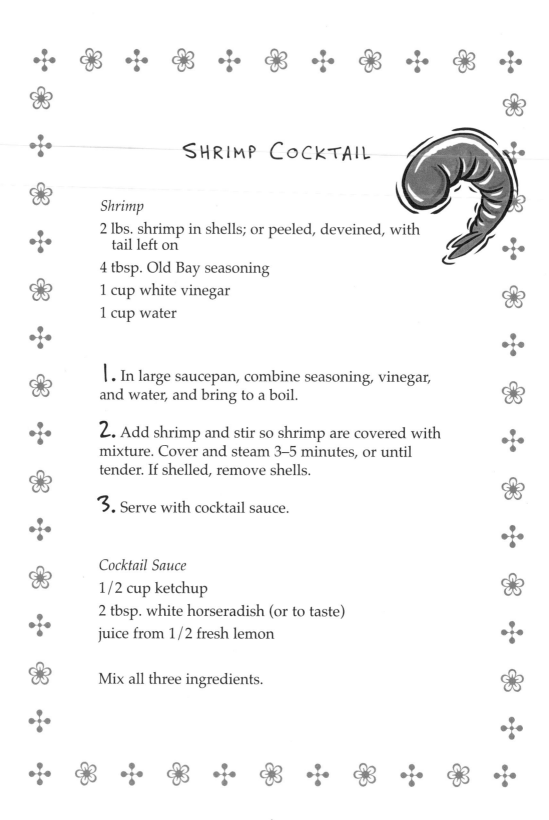

Shrimp

2 lbs. shrimp in shells; or peeled, deveined, with
  tail left on

4 tbsp. Old Bay seasoning

1 cup white vinegar

1 cup water

1. In large saucepan, combine seasoning, vinegar,
and water, and bring to a boil.

2. Add shrimp and stir so shrimp are covered with
mixture. Cover and steam 3–5 minutes, or until
tender. If shelled, remove shells.

3. Serve with cocktail sauce.

Cocktail Sauce

1/2 cup ketchup

2 tbsp. white horseradish (or to taste)

juice from 1/2 fresh lemon

Mix all three ingredients.

Brother David's Baked Stuffed Jalapeños

Makes 50 servings

25 fresh jalapeños, cut in half lengthwise, deveined and deseeded

1 lb. bulk Italian sausage

1/2 cup mozzarella cheese, shredded

1 lb. hot pepper cheese

1. Mix the sausage with the mozzarella and stuff the jalapeño halves.

2. Bake at 350° for 35 minutes, then remove and place a thin slice of hot pepper cheese on each stuffed jalapeño.

3. Return to the oven until cheese melts.

These are nowhere near as hot as you might fear. Deseeding and deveining the peppers takes the hot out.

Sunday Brunches and Everyday Lunches

As often as is practicable there shall be silence in the refectory during the three community meals, together with reading. The matter chosen for reading . . . shall be of an edifying, instructive, and interesting nature.
—Constitution #223

In the beginning of my religious life, the rule of silence at meals was always *practicable*, as was listening carefully since random quizzes were given in Constitution Class on what was read. I suppose silence at meals was also *practical* because the chatter of fifty teenagers would have been unbearable. The sisters chosen to read were those who had pleasant voices, an expressive manner, and were well-regarded by the superior. I was not one of them and for that I was daily grateful. I had a hard time doing anything in silence without laughing, and just the thought of reading to my peers was way beyond my self-control.

Our Superior in the novitiate was a theologian who took great care in selecting readings that were both interesting and instructive. The most memorable was an article by Fr. Anthony Padavano on the vow of poverty and what a paradox it is to be so rich while owning nothing. Fr. Padavano was a prominent theologian at the time and his writings were widely read and highly regarded by everyone in the sisterhood. The novice who read that morning did so with a firm, commanding voice, and unusual dramatic flair. What she felt were profound thoughts were read slowly, even breathlessly, with pauses between sentences for us to reflect on their meaning. Several of us could hardly contain our laughter during the dramatic pauses, and by the end of the article no one could. The final sentence summed up the paradox of being simultaneously poor and rich and said something like, "And this is the perfect enigma. . . ."

Sister Laverne, however, reaching a crescendo of dramatic flair, looked up as if she was about to speak the final words of a Shakespearean play, leaned over the microphone, and whispered slowly, "And . . . this . . . is . . . the . . . perfect . . . enema."

College graduation, 1969.

Sunday Brunches

Eggs Saint Benedict

1 English muffin per person (cut in half)
2 slices Canadian bacon per person, fried
2 poached eggs per person
Hollandaise Sauce

The Perfectly Poached Egg

Always begin with the freshest of eggs.

1. Fill a skillet with about 1 inch of water, add 1 tbsp. white wine vinegar, and heat the water to a simmer—the very gentlest of boils. Keep the flame low enough to maintain a simmer.

2. Gently crack the egg into a saucer, being careful not to break the yolk. Slowly slip the egg from the saucer into the simmering water, then use a slotted spoon to fold the whites over the yolk. Don't worry about scraggly edges.

3. Cook only 1 or 2 eggs at a time. You want the whites to cook firmly while the yolks remain soft to the touch. This takes about 2 minutes, unless you want harder yolks.

4. If serving immediately, carefully remove the egg with a slotted spoon, and blot on the toasted heel from a loaf of bread. Blotting prevents the egg from making the English muffin soggy. It works like a sponge.

5. Place a slice of Canadian bacon on each muffin, then turn the blotted egg back onto the slotted spoon, and slide on top of Canadian bacon.

6. If not serving immediately, poached eggs can be kept in a bowl of ice water, even overnight.

7. Chilled eggs can be reheated in simmering water for 2–3 minutes, then blotted on the bread sponge and served.

8. If so desired you can trim off the scraggly edges. The perfect poached egg looks like a little UFO.

Hollandaise (Sauce of the Gods)
Makes 3/4 cup
3 large egg yolks
1 tbsp. fresh lemon juice
1/2 cup unsalted butter, melted
salt and white pepper, to taste
1/4 cup hot water

Hollandaise is always best made at the last minute and used immediately. You can use a double boiler or a glass bowl over a pot of steaming, not boiling, water.

1. Put the egg yolks in the top of double boiler, and whisk 3-4 minutes, until yolks thicken.

2. Add 1/4 cup hot water to eggs 1 tbsp. at a time, whisking constantly. If the mix starts to curdle add an ice cube and mix till it melts. That will remove the curdles.

3. Slowly dribble melted butter into eggs, continuing to whisk. Add lemon juice and continue whisking until sauce turns pale yellow. Salt and pepper to taste.

4. Spoon sauce over poached eggs and serve.

Eggscellent.

35

EGGS McGUIGAN

Makes 1

1 English muffin
2 slices Canadian bacon
1 egg
1 tbsp. butter
1/4 cup water

1. Toast the English muffin. Keep it warm

2. Microwave or panfry the Canadian bacon. Keep it warm.

3. Steam the egg: Melt 1 tbsp. butter in a small skillet over medium heat. Crack the egg carefully, trying to contain the whites. Break the yolk gently with a fork and lightly scramble just enough to flatten the yolk. Add water to the skillet, then cover and let egg steam 3–4 minutes, or until yolks are firm.

4. While eggs are cooking, lightly butter both halves of the English muffin, and place a slice of hot Canadian bacon on each half.

5. Using a slotted spatula, slide the egg onto half of the muffin, cover with the other half, and serve.

EGG AND SAUSAGE BAKE

1 lb. spicy breakfast sausage
6 large eggs
2 cups milk
1 tsp. salt
1 tsp. dry mustard
6 slices day old white bread, crusts removed
1 cup fresh grated cheddar cheese

1. Fry sausage until light!y browned and crumbly. Drain and set aside.

2. Mix eggs, milk, salt, and dry mustard, and set aside.

3. Break bread into bite-size chunks, mix with cheese, and spread into 8"x12" greased baking dish.

4. Pour the egg mixture over bread, sprinkle sausage on top, cover with foil, and refrigerate overnight.

5. Preheat oven to 350°, and bake 50–60 minutes.

FABULOUS FRENCH TOAST

4 large eggs
1/2 cup half & half
1/4 tsp. vanilla extract
1 tbsp. sugar
1/8 tsp. ground cinnamon
1/8 tsp. ground nutmeg
6 slices stale white bread
unsalted butter for frying

1. With a fork, beat the eggs lightly in a bowl with the half & half. Add vanilla, nutmeg, cinnamon, and sugar. Mix again.

2. Soak each slice of bread in the batter, pressing down with a fork so it soaks up the egg mix.

3. Cook in foaming melted butter over medium flame for 2–3 minutes per side, or until golden brown. Keep adding butter if necessary.

4. Serve with butter, heated maple syrup, or for something extra special, add fresh fruit.

French toast must be made with stale bread—at least two days old. Fresh bread soaks up the egg mixture and gets soggy. Few things are worse than soggy French toast. You want the egg mixture to coat the bread, not kill it. Italian bread is good, challah bread is divine, and even good old Wonder Bread remains a wonder.

BUTTERMILK PANCAKES WITH RASPBERRY SAUCE

Pancakes

1 1/2 cups all-purpose flour

2 tsp. baking soda

1/2 tsp. salt

2 cups buttermilk

6 tbsp. unsalted butter, melted

2 large eggs, room temperature, separated

1. Sift together flour, baking soda, and salt in medium bowl and set aside.

2. In another bowl, mix buttermilk, butter, and egg yolks until blended. Add dry ingredients to buttermilk mix and stir until well blended.

3. Beat egg whites into stiff peaks and fold into pancake batter. Blend well.

4. Cook in lightly buttered skillet over medium flame about 2 minutes, until edges bubble. Flip and cook another 2 minutes or until golden brown.

5. Serve with fresh raspberry sauce.

Raspberry Sauce

4 cups fresh raspberries

1 1/2 cups sugar

1/4 cup water

1. Combine water with raspberries in a saucepan, gently mashing berries with a fork. Cover and bring to a boil over high heat.

2. Strain boiled raspberry mix into a bowl and mix in sugar. Return raspberry puree to pan and boil over high heat until sugar dissolves, about 1–2 minutes. Serve warm.

FRESH BLUEBERRY PANCAKES

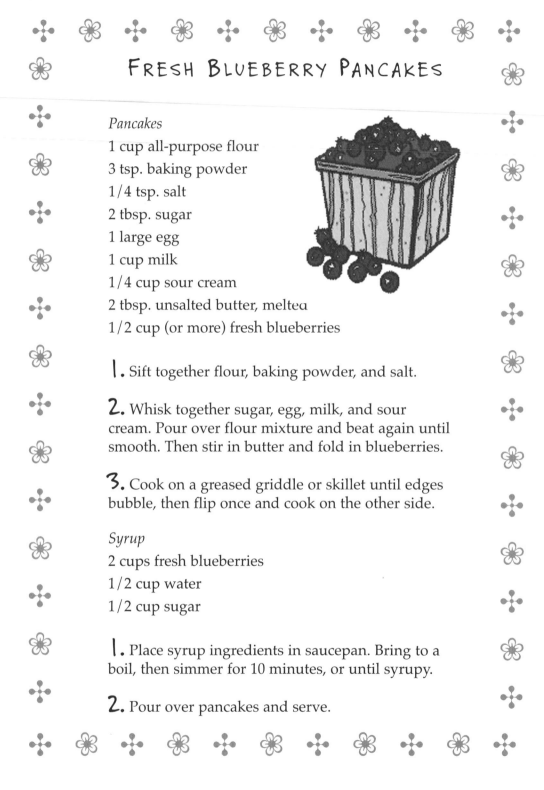

Pancakes

1 cup all-purpose flour

3 tsp. baking powder

1/4 tsp. salt

2 tbsp. sugar

1 large egg

1 cup milk

1/4 cup sour cream

2 tbsp. unsalted butter, melted

1/2 cup (or more) fresh blueberries

1. Sift together flour, baking powder, and salt.

2. Whisk together sugar, egg, milk, and sour cream. Pour over flour mixture and beat again until smooth. Then stir in butter and fold in blueberries.

3. Cook on a greased griddle or skillet until edges bubble, then flip once and cook on the other side.

Syrup

2 cups fresh blueberries

1/2 cup water

1/2 cup sugar

1. Place syrup ingredients in saucepan. Bring to a boil, then simmer for 10 minutes, or until syrupy.

2. Pour over pancakes and serve.

Sinfully Good Sinnamon Rolls

3/4 cup sugar
1 1/2 cups dark brown sugar
dash of ground nutmeg
2 tsp. ground cinnamon
1/3 cup finely chopped walnuts or pecans
1/2 cup unsalted butter, melted
1/2 cup heavy cream
2 loaves white bread dough

1. Mix sugars, nutmeg, cinnamon, and nuts in small bowl and set aside.

2. Over low flame, blend the butter and cream, stirring constantly until smooth and creamy. Pour into a 9"x13" glass baking dish and set aside.

3. Take one loaf of the white bread dough and spread out into a 5"x12" rectangle on a lightly floured pastry cloth or a floured, clean surface.

4. Sprinkle with half of the nut mixture, roll it up, and cut into three pieces. Do the same with the other loaf.

5. Place the cinnamon spins in the baking dish on top of the cream mixture. Cover with a cloth and let rise in a warm place until they double in size (about 1 hour).

6. Bake at 350° for 30 minutes, or until golden brown. Remove and let cool 15–20 minutes before turning over onto a platter and serving.

BUTTERMILK BISCUITS
WITH OR WITHOUT GRAVY

Makes about 12

Biscuits

2 cups all-purpose flour	3 tbsp. shortening
1/4 tsp. baking soda	3 tbsp. unsalted butter
1 tbsp. baking powder	1 cup buttermilk
1 tsp. salt	

1. Sift dry ingredients in a big bowl, then cut in the shortening and butter until the mixture looks like coarse meal. Add the buttermilk and mix everything together by hand. Add flour if it gets too sticky.

2. Knead dough for 1 minute, or until dough forms into a ball.

3. Wrap in wax paper and refrigerate until well chilled, approximately 15–20 minutes.

4. Roll out dough on lightly floured pastry cloth 1/2-inch thick, then use a 2-inch biscuit cutter or a glass to cut the dough into circles. Re-roll the scrap dough to make as many biscuits as possible.

5. Arrange the biscuits on an ungreased, non-stick baking sheet. It's okay if they touch. Bake 10–12 minutes, or until golden brown.

> There are three secrets to a good light biscuit: don't over-knead the dough, don't use too much flour when rolling out the dough, and always bake in a very hot preheated oven (450°).

Sausage Gravy

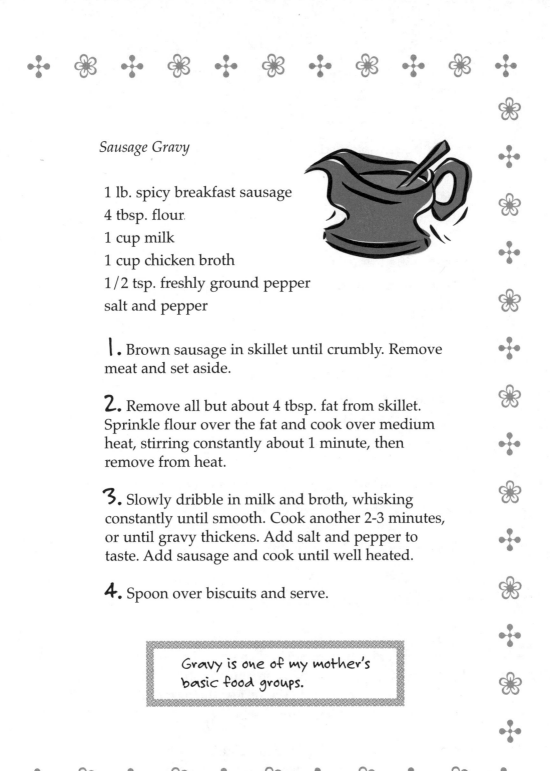

1 lb. spicy breakfast sausage
4 tbsp. flour
1 cup milk
1 cup chicken broth
1/2 tsp. freshly ground pepper
salt and pepper

1. Brown sausage in skillet until crumbly. Remove meat and set aside.

2. Remove all but about 4 tbsp. fat from skillet. Sprinkle flour over the fat and cook over medium heat, stirring constantly about 1 minute, then remove from heat.

3. Slowly dribble in milk and broth, whisking constantly until smooth. Cook another 2-3 minutes, or until gravy thickens. Add salt and pepper to taste. Add sausage and cook until well heated.

4. Spoon over biscuits and serve.

Gravy is one of my mother's basic food groups.

Sour Cream Coffee Cake

1 cup butter, softened
2 cups sugar
2 large eggs
1 cup sour cream
1 1/2 tsp. vanilla extract
2 cups sifted flour
1 tsp. baking powder
1/4 tsp. salt

Topping
1/2 cup chopped walnuts or pecans
1/2 cup brown sugar
1/2 cup white sugar
1 tbsp. ground cinnamon

1. Beat butter and sugar until well blended. Add eggs, sour cream, and vanilla and keep beating. Gradually add flour, baking powder, and salt. Mix until well blended and creamy.

2. Make the topping by combining the nuts, sugars, and cinnamon in a small bowl. Set aside.

3. Lightly grease and flour an 8- or 10-inch springform bundt pan. Sprinkle half of the topping on the bottom of the pan. Then spread half of the batter in the pan, sprinkle the rest of the topping over the batter, and add the rest of the batter.

4. Bake at 350° for 1 hour, or until top is golden brown. Cool for 15 minutes, then turn onto plate.

CRANBERRY NUT BREAD

2 cups all-purpose flour

3/4 cup sugar

1 tsp. baking powder

1/4 tsp. baking soda

1 tsp. salt

2/3 cup fresh squeezed orange juice

1/2 cup buttermilk

2 eggs, beaten lightly

4 tbsp. unsalted butter, melted

1/2 cup pecans or walnuts, coarsely chopped

1 1/2 cups fresh cranberries

1 tbsp. grated orange rind

1. Sift flour, sugar, baking powder, baking soda, and salt in mixing bowl.

2. Make a well in the middle of the flour mixture and pour in orange juice, buttermilk, eggs, and butter. Mix well, but don't over mix; then fold in pecans, cranberries, and orange rind.

3. Grease a loaf pan, then pour in batter. Place on the middle rack of 350° preheated oven. Bake 50–60 minutes, until top is golden brown and a toothpick inserted in the middle comes out clean.

4. Cool in the pan for 10 minutes before removing, then let cool on the rack for an hour before serving. It's even better if you wrap it for a day or two before serving.

Everyday Lunches

SHIRL'S SLOPPY JOES

2 lbs. ground chuck
1 large onion, finely chopped
2 stalks celery, finely chopped
1 green pepper, finely chopped
1 large garlic clove, minced
1 tbsp. vinegar
1/2 tsp. salt
2 tbsp. sugar
2 tbsp. mustard
1 tsp. freshly ground pepper
1/4 tsp. cayenne pepper, if you like it spicy
1 cup ketchup

1. Cook ground chuck until browned. Then mix in onion, celery, green pepper, and garlic, and simmer 10 minutes.

2. Drain grease, then add remaining ingredients. Mix well and simmer partially covered for 1 hour. Add water if necessary, or cook uncovered if too watery.

3. Serve on hamburger buns. It's even better if refrigerated overnight and eaten the next day.

ITALIAN SAUSAGE AND PEPPERS

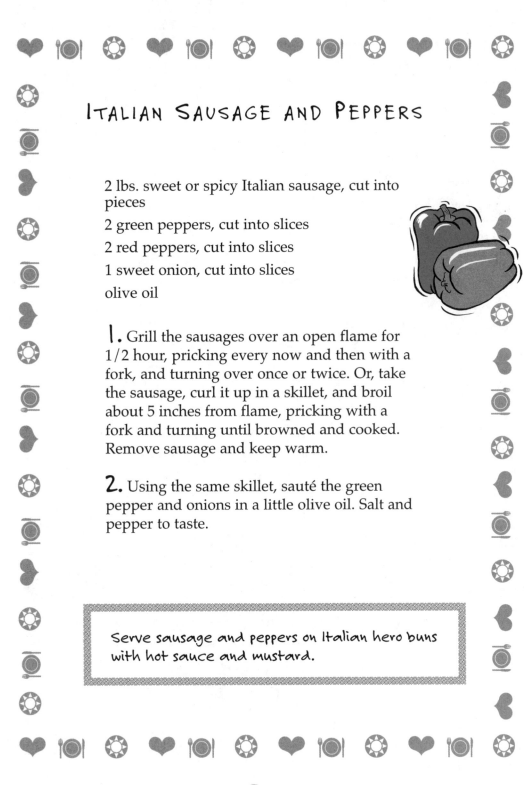

2 lbs. sweet or spicy Italian sausage, cut into pieces
2 green peppers, cut into slices
2 red peppers, cut into slices
1 sweet onion, cut into slices
olive oil

1. Grill the sausages over an open flame for 1/2 hour, pricking every now and then with a fork, and turning over once or twice. Or, take the sausage, curl it up in a skillet, and broil about 5 inches from flame, pricking with a fork and turning until browned and cooked. Remove sausage and keep warm.

2. Using the same skillet, sauté the green pepper and onions in a little olive oil. Salt and pepper to taste.

Serve sausage and peppers on Italian hero buns with hot sauce and mustard.

World's Best Chili

2 cups dried pinto beans
6 cups canned plum tomatoes
1 cup green pepper, finely chopped
2 cups onion, finely chopped
2 tbsp. vegetable oil
4 garlic cloves, crushed
1/2 cup parsley, finely chopped
1/3 cup chili powder

2 tbsp. salt
1 tsp. cayenne pepper
1 tbsp. freshly ground pepper
1 tbsp. red pepper flakes
1/4 cup Dijon mustard
2 1/2 lbs. ground chuck
1 lb. ground pork

1. Wash pinto beans and soak overnight in water 3 inches above the beans.

2. In a large chili pot, simmer the beans until water is absorbed. Then add tomatoes, and simmer 10 minutes more.

3. Sauté green pepper and onion in vegetable oil for 5 minutes. Stir in garlic and parsley, then add ingredients to chili pot.

4. Blend in the chili powder, salt, cayenne pepper, pepper, red pepper flakes, and mustard. Mix well and continue to simmer.

5. Cook meats together in skillet until brown. Drain and add to chili pot.

6. Cover partially and simmer on medium to low flame for 1 hour, stirring every 15 minutes. Then uncover, and simmer 30 minutes more.

7. Serve with shredded cheddar cheese, sour cream, jalapeños, oyster crackers, and chopped onion.

SHEPHERD'S PIE

7 Idaho potatoes
1 cup half and half (warm)
1/4 cup butter, soft
salt and freshly ground black pepper
3 lbs. ground beef
1 cup onion, finely chopped
2 cups corn kernels
2 cups diced cooked carrots
2 cups green peas

1. Boil potatoes, drain, and mash very fine with cream and butter. Salt and pepper to taste.

2. Cook ground beef, adding onion, salt, and pepper.

3. Drain cooked meat and spread in 9"x13" baking dish. Cover with corn, carrots, and peas, and stir until blended.

4. Spread mashed potatoes over the meat mixture and bake at 375° for 30 minutes, or until potatoes begin to brown.

You can substitute cooked lentils for the ground beef if you like vegetarian fare.

MACARONI AND CHEESE

1/2 lb. elbow or shell macaroni
1/2 tsp. salt
2 eggs
1-12 oz. can evaporated milk, heated
1 tsp. yellow mustard
4 tbsp. unsalted butter
freshly ground pepper, to taste; I like lots
2 cups mild cheddar cheese, grated
1 cup Monterey Jack cheese, grated
1 cup fontina cheese, grated

1. Cook macaroni as directed (should be tender but firm). Drain into 2-quart baking dish and stir in butter until melted.

2. Whisk together the eggs, milk, mustard, salt, and pepper. Pour over macaroni and stir.

3. Blend the cheeses and mix in well with macaroni.

4. Bake at 350° for 40 minutes, removing to stir after 20 minutes. If you like toasted breadcrumbs or something else on top, add for the last 20 minutes.

5. Or, skip the sauce. Layer the mac and cheese. Salt and pepper each layer, with a cheese layer on top. Pour milk over all. Bake at 350° for 40 minutes until top browns and cheese bubbles.

> Either way it's divine.

MARRY ME EGG SALAD SANDWICH

4 hard-boiled eggs

3 tsp. onion, diced extremely fine (that's the
  secret)

3 tbsp. mayonnaise

salt and pepper to taste

white dinner rolls or Wonder Bread

1. In a small bowl, mash eggs with a fork.

2. Soak onion in water for five minutes to remove
heat, then dice fine.

3. Add mayonnaise, onion, salt, and pepper. Mix
until everything is evenly coated with mayonnaise.

4. Serve on white dinner rolls or Wonder Bread.

> The "Me" that got married over this egg
> salad was Brenda Bent, not me.

New Orleans Red Beans and Rice

Serves 8

1 lb. red kidney beans

1 lb. andouille sausage (or pepperoni), sliced

1 large onion, chopped

2 cloves garlic, chopped

1/2 cup celery, chopped

ham bone with a lot of meat

1 bay leaf

dash of cayenne pepper

1 tsp. hot pepper sauce

6 cups cooked white rice

1. Cover beans with water and soak overnight.

2. In a deep pan, sauté sausage, onion, garlic, and celery until sausage is slightly browned. Add beans with the water in which they've been soaking, then the ham bone. Add more water to cover. Then add bay leaf, cayenne, and hot sauce to taste. Cook over medium to low heat for 2–3 hours.

3. Spoon over cooked rice and serve with cornbread.

Cornbread

2/3 cup oil or bacon drippings

2 eggs

2 1/2 cups milk

2 cups cornmeal

2 cups all-purpose flour

2 tbsp. baking powder

3 tsp. baking soda

1 tsp. salt

1. In a large bowl, add oil and eggs, then beat until foamy. Add milk and blend well.

2. Sift in dry ingredients, and mix again until well blended.

3. Pour batter into a very hot, well greased cast iron skillet (or muffin tin for 12 muffins), and bake at 475° for 20 minutes.

CHICKEN TACOS

3 garlic cloves, crushed
1 tsp. salt
1 tbsp. vegetable oil
1 large onion, chopped
1 large tomato, seeded and chopped
1-6 oz. can chopped green chilis
1/2 tsp. ground cumin

hot sauce, to taste
4 cups shredded cooked chicken
12 taco shells, hard or soft
shredded lettuce
grated cheddar cheese
sour cream

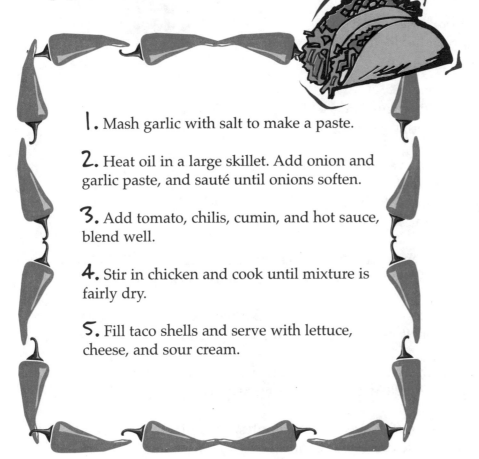

1. Mash garlic with salt to make a paste.

2. Heat oil in a large skillet. Add onion and garlic paste, and sauté until onions soften.

3. Add tomato, chilis, cumin, and hot sauce, blend well.

4. Stir in chicken and cook until mixture is fairly dry.

5. Fill taco shells and serve with lettuce, cheese, and sour cream.

Asparagus Quiche

Serves 5

1 lb. fresh asparagus, trimmed

1-9 inch pie shell, unbaked (usually in the dairy section of the supermarket)

3 tbsp. butter

3 tbsp. flour

1/2 tsp. salt

1 1/2 cups milk

4 eggs, beaten

1/2 cup shredded Swiss cheese

1 tsp. dried dill

1. Cut asparagus into 1/2-inch pieces. Cook in a small amount of water, drain, set aside.

2. Preheat oven to 450°. Line unpricked pie shell with double thickness foil and bake 5 minutes. Remove foil and bake 5 minutes more. Remove from oven and set aside. Reduce oven temperature to 400°.

3. In saucepan, melt butter over medium heat, then stir in flour and salt. Add milk gradually, stirring until thickened.

4. Blend a small amount of the mixture in with the eggs, then add egg mixture to saucepan, stirring to blend.

5. Add cheese, asparagus pieces, and dill, stirring to blend. Pour into crust. Steps 4 and 5 go very quickly.

6. Bake in a 400° oven for 35 minutes, or until a knife inserted in the middle comes out clean.

CRAB CAKES

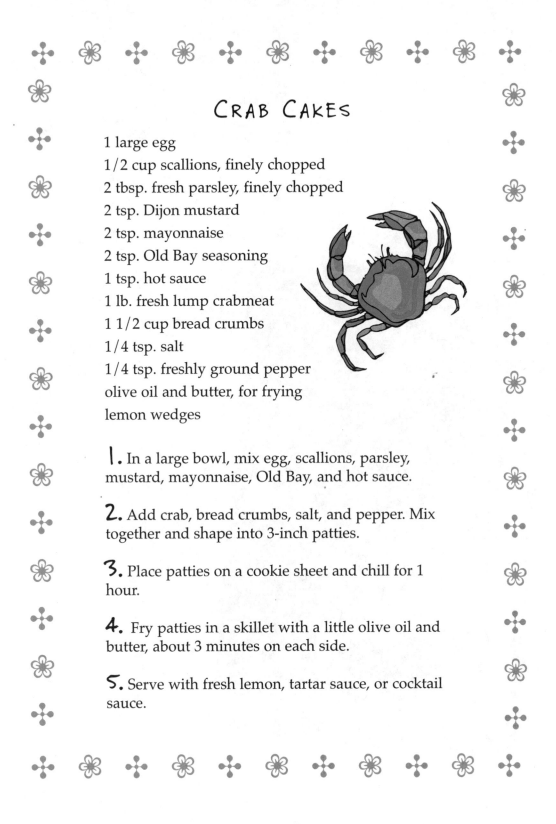

1 large egg
1/2 cup scallions, finely chopped
2 tbsp. fresh parsley, finely chopped
2 tsp. Dijon mustard
2 tsp. mayonnaise
2 tsp. Old Bay seasoning
1 tsp. hot sauce
1 lb. fresh lump crabmeat
1 1/2 cup bread crumbs
1/4 tsp. salt
1/4 tsp. freshly ground pepper
olive oil and butter, for frying
lemon wedges

1. In a large bowl, mix egg, scallions, parsley, mustard, mayonnaise, Old Bay, and hot sauce.

2. Add crab, bread crumbs, salt, and pepper. Mix together and shape into 3-inch patties.

3. Place patties on a cookie sheet and chill for 1 hour.

4. Fry patties in a skillet with a little olive oil and butter, about 3 minutes on each side.

5. Serve with fresh lemon, tartar sauce, or cocktail sauce.

Soulful Soups
and Salads

The sisters shall be content with what is served at the table. The meals shall be simple, and of sufficient abundance to maintain the sisters in good health and enable them to perform their duties.
—Constitution #219

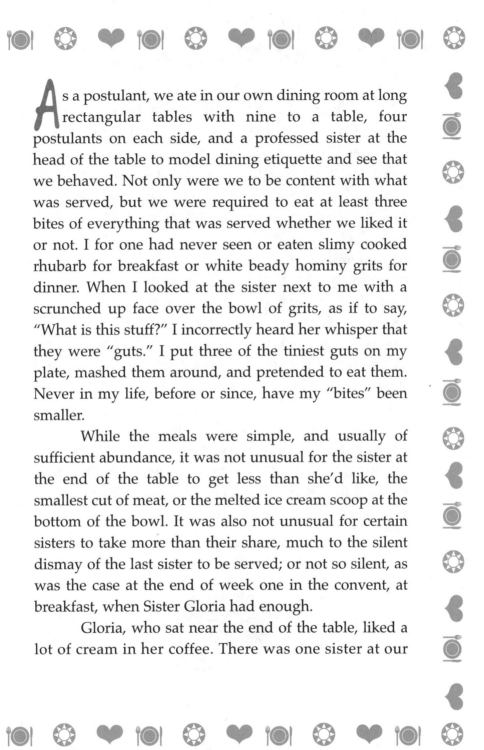

As a postulant, we ate in our own dining room at long rectangular tables with nine to a table, four postulants on each side, and a professed sister at the head of the table to model dining etiquette and see that we behaved. Not only were we to be content with what was served, but we were required to eat at least three bites of everything that was served whether we liked it or not. I for one had never seen or eaten slimy cooked rhubarb for breakfast or white beady hominy grits for dinner. When I looked at the sister next to me with a scrunched up face over the bowl of grits, as if to say, "What is this stuff?" I incorrectly heard her whisper that they were "guts." I put three of the tiniest guts on my plate, mashed them around, and pretended to eat them. Never in my life, before or since, have my "bites" been smaller.

While the meals were simple, and usually of sufficient abundance, it was not unusual for the sister at the end of the table to get less than she'd like, the smallest cut of meat, or the melted ice cream scoop at the bottom of the bowl. It was also not unusual for certain sisters to take more than their share, much to the silent dismay of the last sister to be served; or not so silent, as was the case at the end of week one in the convent, at breakfast, when Sister Gloria had enough.

Gloria, who sat near the end of the table, liked a lot of cream in her coffee. There was one sister at our table who proudly poured all the remaining cream in her coffee every day, then handed Gloria the empty container. This went on for three days, and each day I could feel Gloria getting madder and madder. She'd bang the empty creamer on the table, ignoring the glare from the professed sister indicating that we just didn't do that.

On day four, I could feel the tension in Gloria mounting quickly as the cream was passed. And true to form, the same sister proceeded to pour every last bit of cream into her cup with a big self-satisfied grin, and to hand the empty container to Gloria. That did it. Gloria took the container, slammed it on the table, turned to the smug sister, and yelled to her face, "YOU COW!"

I'd venture to say that every sister who had to sit at the end of the table wanted to do to some sister what Gloria did that morning. Needless to say she remains a heroic figure in my life, and she left me with a memory that still makes me laugh. Gloria Glaser, wherever you are, I thank you.

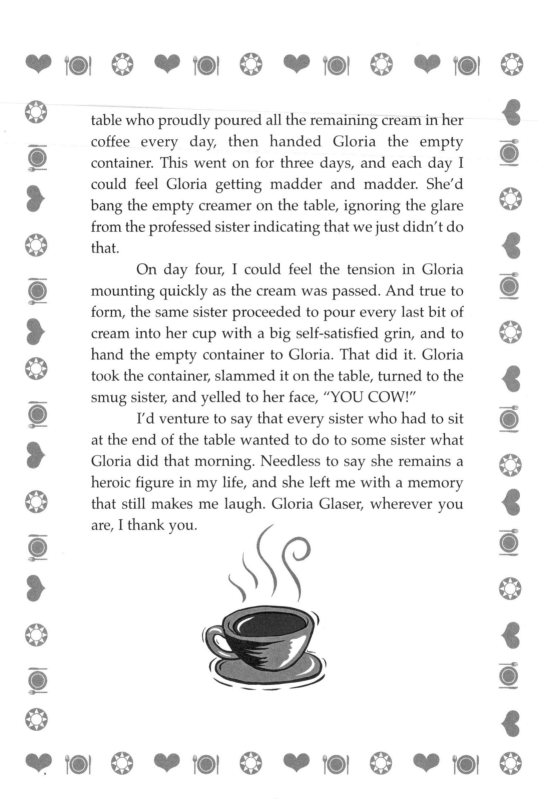

Soulful Soups

CORN CHOWDER

Serves 6

6 slices bacon, cut into 1-inch pieces

2 tbsp. unsalted butter

2 cups onion, finely chopped

2 garlic cloves, finely minced

2 tbsp. all-purpose flour

3 cups chicken stock

2 red skinned potatoes, peeled and cut into bite-size chunks

1 cup half and half

2 cups milk

4 cups cooked corn kernels, preferably fresh corn (about 12 ears)

cayenne pepper, just a dash

1 tsp. freshly ground pepper

1 tsp. salt

2 tbsp. fresh parsley, chopped

salt and freshly ground pepper, to taste

1. Fry bacon in a large soup pot over low heat about 5 minutes, just until fat is rendered. Add butter and let it melt.

2. Over low heat, add onion and garlic, sauté for 10 minutes, then stir in flour and cook another 5 minutes.

3. Pour in chicken stock and add potatoes, cooking over medium heat until potatoes are tender, about 15–20 minutes.

4. Add half and half, milk, corn, cayenne pepper, freshly ground pepper, and salt, and cook over low heat for another 10 minutes, stirring constantly, making sure it doesn't boil. Stir in parsley, salt, and pepper to taste.

CREAM OF MUSHROOM SOUP

Makes 4 servings

1/2 lb. mushrooms

4 tbsp. unsalted butter

1 med. onion, finely
  chopped

1/4 cup all-purpose flour

1 tsp. salt

1/2 tsp. freshly ground
  pepper

1/4 cup water

1 can chicken broth

1 cup half and half

fresh parsley, chopped for
  garnish

1. Slice enough mushrooms to measure 1 cup, and chop the rest.

2. Melt 2 tbsp. butter in a large saucepan and sauté 1 cup sliced mushrooms over low heat until golden brown. Then remove with slotted spoon and set aside.

3. Add rest of the butter to pot with onion and chopped mushrooms, cooking until onion is tender. Then stir in flour, salt, and pepper, cooking over low heat, stirring constantly for about 1 minute.

4. Remove from heat and stir in water and chicken broth. Return to heat and bring to a boil, stirring constantly for about 1 minute.

5. Stir in half and half and sliced mushrooms, heating just until hot. Do not boil. Garnish with parsley and serve.

MARY FEELEY'S FRENCH ONION SOUP

Makes 6 servings

1 1/2 lbs. onion, thinly sliced
3 tbsp. butter
1 tbsp. oil
1 tsp. salt
1/4 tsp. sugar
3 tbsp. flour
2 qts. beef stock
1/2 cup dry vermouth
salt and pepper, to taste
6 tsp. cognac
1 cup Swiss or Gruyere cheese, grated

1. In medium saucepan and over a low heat blend butter and oil then add onions. Cover pan and cook for 15 minutes.

2. Uncover, raise heat to medium, and stir in salt and sugar. This helps brown the onions. Cook for 35–40 minutes, stirring frequently until the onions turn deep and golden brown.

3. Stir in flour and simmer for 3 minutes.

4. In another pot, bring 2 quarts of beef stock to a boil. Blend onions into boiling stock, then add vermouth and season with salt and pepper. Simmer, partially covered, for 40 minutes. Skim to remove fat.

Just before serving stir in cognac. Serve with grated cheese. You can also preheat the broiler, or the oven to 350°. Divide soup into ovenproof bowls and melt the cheese.

> The onions need a long, slow cooking in butter and oil, then a long, slow simmering in stock for them to develop the deep rich flavor which characterizes a perfect brew.

COMFORTING SPLIT PEA SOUP

Makes 6 servings

1 lb. dried green split peas
5 cups chicken stock
5 cups water
3 smoked ham hocks
1/2 cup celery, finely chopped
4 tbsp. unsalted butter
1 cup onion, finely chopped
1 cup carrots, finely chopped
4 large cloves garlic, minced
1 tsp. freshly ground pepper

1. In a large soup pot, combine peas with stock and water and bring to a boil.

2. Add ham hocks and celery, then reduce heat to medium-low and simmer partially covered for 45 minutes.

3. Melt the butter in a saucepan over medium heat and sauté onion, carrots, and garlic about 10 minutes. Then add them to the soup pot, and simmer, partially covered, for another 30 minutes.

4. Remove the soup from heat. Take out ham hocks and remove the meat from the bone. Return the meat to the soup, add pepper, reheat to boiling point, then serve.

FRIDAY'S TOMATO SOUP

Makes 8 servings

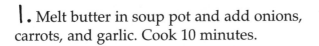

1/4 cup unsalted butter
2 small onions, thinly sliced
2 large carrots, peeled and chopped
3 cloves garlic, minced
2-35 oz. cans plum tomatoes, with juice
pinch of sugar
4 large fresh basil leaves, slivered
salt and freshly ground pepper to taste
4 cups chicken stock
2 cups heavy cream

1. Melt butter in soup pot and add onions, carrots, and garlic. Cook 10 minutes.

2. Add tomatoes with juice, sugar, basil, salt, and pepper, and cook 5 minutes. Then add stock and bring to a boil. Reduce heat, partially cover, and cook another 45 minutes.

3. Puree the soup in a food processor, return it to the pot, add the cream, and reheat until hot but not boiling.

> Nearly every Friday, in nearly every convent in the world, lunch consisted of canned tomato soup and grilled cheese sandwiches. I hated tomato soup until I tasted this one.

CHEDDAR CHEESE SOUP

Serves 4–6

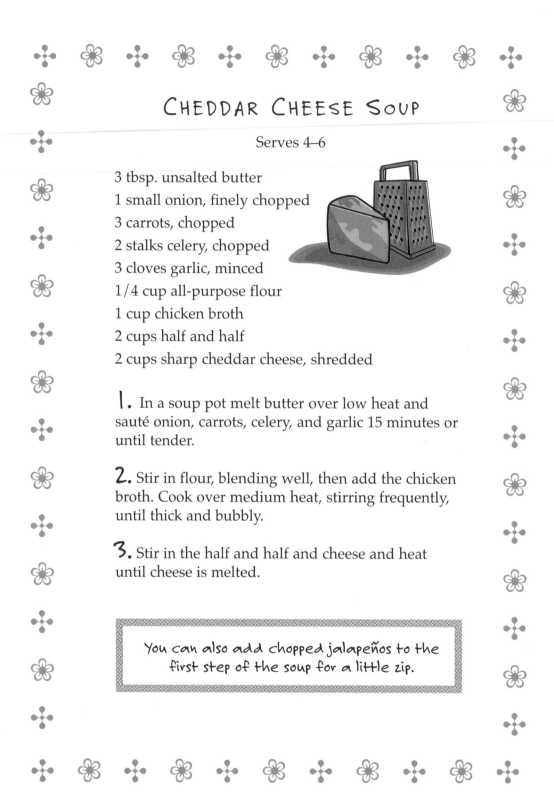

3 tbsp. unsalted butter
1 small onion, finely chopped
3 carrots, chopped
2 stalks celery, chopped
3 cloves garlic, minced
1/4 cup all-purpose flour
1 cup chicken broth
2 cups half and half
2 cups sharp cheddar cheese, shredded

1. In a soup pot melt butter over low heat and sauté onion, carrots, celery, and garlic 15 minutes or until tender.

2. Stir in flour, blending well, then add the chicken broth. Cook over medium heat, stirring frequently, until thick and bubbly.

3. Stir in the half and half and cheese and heat until cheese is melted.

> You can also add chopped jalapeños to the first step of the soup for a little zip.

Soulful Salads

THE BEST CAESAR SALAD

Serves 8

2 heads Romaine lettuce

2 eggs, lightly beaten

4 garlic cloves, crushed

6 tbsp. fresh squeezed lemon juice

1 cup olive oil

4 hard-boiled eggs, quartered

6 anchovies, drained and chopped (optional)

1 cup freshly grated Parmesan cheese

2 cups seasoned croutons

freshly ground pepper, to taste

grilled chicken breast or grilled shrimp (optional)

1. Separate and clean lettuce leaves. Wrap in paper towel and refrigerate several hours to crisp the leaves.

2. In a large salad bowl, whisk together raw egg, garlic, lemon juice, and olive oil.

3. Add lettuce, hard-boiled eggs, and anchovies, then toss well with dressing. Add Parmesan cheese and toss again. Sprinkle with croutons and serve immediately with freshly ground pepper. (Grilled chicken and shrimp can be added at this point, making this a meal in itself.)

GREEK PASTA SALAD

2 cups ruffled pasta, cooked and drained
2 cups chicken, cooked and cubed (optional)
1/2 pint cherry tomatoes, cut in half
1 large cucumber, cut lengthwise and sliced
1/2 large red onion, coarsely chopped
3 tbsp. fresh lemon juice
2 tsp. salt
1/2 cup olive oil
1 1/2 tsp. dried oregano
6 oz. feta cheese, crumbled
1/2 cup Greek olives, sliced

1. In a large bowl, combine cooked pasta, chicken, tomatoes, cucumber, and onion.

2. In a small bowl, mix lemon juice and salt until salt dissolves; add olive oil and oregano and stir to blend. Add to pasta and mix well.

3. Add feta cheese and olives. Toss gently to mix.

4. Cover and refrigerate at least two hours, better yet, overnight.

RITA BURNS' THREE "P" SALAD

2 cups frozen **p**eas, cooked and cooled

1 1/2 cups Spanish **p**eanuts, salted, but without skins

1 cup sweet **p**ickles, chopped

2 cups cheddar or American cheese, cut into tiny chunks

mayonnaise, to taste

1. Mix the three **P**s together with the cheese chunks. Add mayonnaise.

2. Chill and serve.

> The salad that made Valley Falls, Kansas famous. All three blocks of it.

67

EVERYBODY'S THREE "B" SALAD

1 can string **b**eans

1 can wax **b**eans

1 can kidney **b**eans

1 large red onion, coarsely
chopped

1 cup celery, diced

3/4 cup oil

3/4 cup sugar

1/4 cup white vinegar

1 tsp. salt

1 tsp. freshly ground pepper

garbanzo beans (optional; makes
it a four "**b**" salad)

Drain beans and mix in big bowl with other ingredients.

Let it sit overnight before serving.

> That's a lot of B.S. (bean salad).

MOM'S POTATO SALAD

10 red-skinned potatoes

2 tbsp. vinegar

8 hard-boiled eggs, chopped

as much celery as you like, finely
chopped

as much green onion as you like,
chopped

salt and freshly ground pepper to
taste

as much mayonnaise as you like
with a little yellow mustard
mixed in, to taste.

1. Boil potatoes until tender, then peel and cut into bite-size chunks.

2. Sprinkle vinegar over potatoes and mix. Then add egg, celery, and onion, and mix again. Season with salt and pepper and mix yet again.

3. Add mayonnaise-mustard mix and toss until all potatoes are well coated. Chill and serve.

> O Momma.

68

MABLE DAVIES' COLE SLAW

3 cups shredded cabbage
1 cup shredded carrots
1/2 cup mayonnaise
1/2 cup sweet pickle juice
celery seed, to taste (optional)

1. Mix together cabbage and carrots (this ratio should look like the Colonel's!).

2. Add mayonnaise, sweet pickle juice (right from the jar), and a little celery seed, if you want.

Mable Davies is from Winnipeg, Canada, which adds an international flair to this cookbook. She's also the mother of Sally Davies, maker of the world's best margaritas.

CRAB LOUIS

Makes 8 servings

Salad

2 lbs. fresh lump crabmeat
1 1/2 cups celery, diced
2 heads iceberg lettuce; leaves separated, rinsed, and dried
4 hard-boiled eggs, cut in half lengthwise
2 tbsp. chopped parsley, for garnish

Dressing

1 cup mayonnaise
1/4 cup chili sauce
1/2 cup sour cream
2 tbsp. fresh lemon juice
1/4 cup green pepper, diced
4 tbsp. chopped green onion
2 tbsp. fresh chives, chopped fine
salt and freshly ground pepper, to taste

1. Combine all the dressing ingredients in a small bowl.

2. Combine the crabmeat, celery and dressing. Blend well.

3. To serve, select cup-shaped lettuce leaves and arrange on salad plate. Fill each leaf with 1/2 cup crab salad. Top with an upside-down egg half and sprinkle with parsley.

> Divine.

WALDORF SALAD

6 Granny Smith apples, peeled and cut into
   bite- size chunks

3 cups celery, finely diced

1 1/2 cups walnuts, finely chopped

3/4 cup mayonnaise

3 tbsp. sugar

3 tbsp. fresh lemon juice

1 tsp. salt

1 1/2 cups fresh whipped cream

1. Combine apples, celery, and nuts.

2. Mix mayonnaise, sugar, lemon juice, and salt. Then fold in whipped cream. Add apples and mix well.

3. Chill and serve on lettuce or off.

FIRST COMMUNION SALAD

16 oz. sour cream

1-10 oz. can mandarin oranges, drained

1-10 oz. can pineapple chunks, with juice

1 cup miniature marshmallows

1 cup flaked coconut

1. Mix everything and let sit in the fridge overnight before serving.

2. You can also add chopped pecans before serving, but my mom didn't.

> I ate nearly a whole bowl of this
> on May 6, 1956, my First Holy Communion.

WILTED SPINACH SALAD

Makes 4 servings

6 cups baby spinach, washed and dried
2 slices bacon, cut into 1/4-inch pieces
1 tbsp. extra virgin olive oil
1/2 cup red onion, chopped fine
1/4 tsp. freshly ground pepper
1/4 tsp. salt
1/4 tsp. sugar
1 tbsp. balsamic vinegar

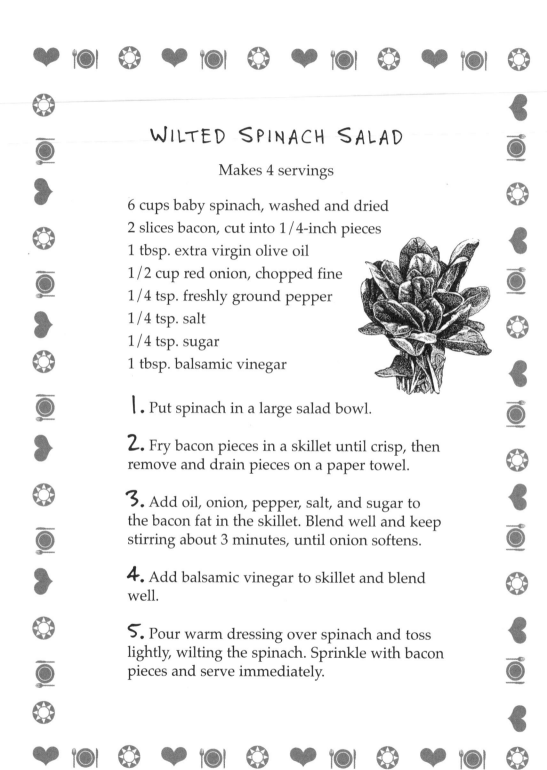

1. Put spinach in a large salad bowl.

2. Fry bacon pieces in a skillet until crisp, then remove and drain pieces on a paper towel.

3. Add oil, onion, pepper, salt, and sugar to the bacon fat in the skillet. Blend well and keep stirring about 3 minutes, until onion softens.

4. Add balsamic vinegar to skillet and blend well.

5. Pour warm dressing over spinach and toss lightly, wilting the spinach. Sprinkle with bacon pieces and serve immediately.

Brown Derby Salad

Makes 6 servings

Salad

1 head Boston lettuce, shredded

2 chicken breasts, cooked, chilled, and diced

2 medium tomatoes, seeded and diced

4 hard-boiled eggs, chopped

8 slices of bacon, fried crisp and crumbled

4 oz. Roquefort cheese, crumbled

2 avocados, peeled, halved lengthwise, and sliced into thin wedges

Dressing

1/2 cup red wine vinegar

1 tbsp. fresh lemon juice

1 tsp. salt

1 tsp. freshly ground pepper

1/2 tsp. sugar

1 1/2 tsp. Worcestershire sauce

1/2 tsp. dry mustard

1 large clove garlic, minced

1 cup olive oil

1. Combine dressing ingredients in a blender or food processor.

2. Put the shredded lettuce in a big salad bowl. On top, arrange a row of chicken, tomatoes, eggs, bacon, and cheese, then surround with avocado slices.

3. Pour the dressing over the salad, tossing the salad until well mixed. Serve on salad plates.

THE SEVEN STORY MOUNTAIN SALAD

Serves 8

Salad

1 head Boston lettuce, shredded

1 cucumber, thinly sliced

1-10 oz. package frozen peas, cooked and cooled

1 lb. bacon, fried crisp and crumbled

1 large red onion, sliced thin

4 hard-boiled eggs, chopped

3 large tomatoes, seeded and diced

12 fresh mushrooms, sliced

1 cup cheddar cheese, grated

Dressing

1 cup mayonnaise

1 cup sour cream

1 tbsp. sugar

1. Blend the mayonnaise, sugar, and sour cream well and set aside.

2. In a large, clear glass trifle bowl put shredded lettuce, then layer the seven stories of ingredients, topping each layer with a little of the dressing mix. Then cover the top of the salad with dressing mix, then the grated cheddar cheese.

3. Cover with plastic wrap and refrigerate until ready to serve.

4. When serving time arrives, toss everything well and serve on salad plates.

Favorite Dressings
for Any Salad

Thousand Island
Makes about 1 1/2 cups
1 hard-boiled egg, chopped
1 cup mayonnaise
1/4 cup chili sauce
3 tbsp. green olives with pimentos, finely chopped
2 tbsp. sweet pickles, finely chopped
1 tbsp. onion, finely chopped
2 tsp. fresh parsley, finely chopped
1 tsp. fresh lemon juice
salt and freshly ground pepper to taste

Combine everything in a mixing bowl and blend well. Salt and pepper to taste.

Creamy Blue Cheese
Makes 3/4 cup
1/2 cup blue cheese, crumbled
3 tbsp. buttermilk
3 tbsp. sour cream
2 tbsp. mayonnaise
2 tsp. white wine vinegar
1/4 tsp. sugar
1/8 tsp. garlic powder
salt and fresh ground pepper, to taste

Mash the blue cheese with the buttermilk, then blend in the rest of the ingredients. Season to taste with salt and pepper.

Divine Dinners and Sides

Conversational powers are no common gift, especially among women meeting daily in the same circle. Every sister shall go to recreation with a view to improve the social spirit of the community and to make all around her happy, that they may experience how good and pleasant it is for sisters to dwell together.

—Constitution #212

Because we were entirely dependent upon ourselves for any kind of recreation, talent shows became a major source of entertainment for special occasions, like Christmas. As postulants, talent shows were also intended to divert attention from how homesick we were. Everyone was expected to do something in the Christmas talent show. I sang Polish Christmas carols with Mary Ann Pajakowski. Some sisters played guitars and sang favorite folk songs. Sister Lucy played her flute. But still, as you can imagine, none of it was enough to divert attention from how homesick we were. That is, until Sister Helene sang a song she composed for the occasion.

In order to understand Helene's Christmas carol you should know that when we entered the convent, razors were not allowed. Those of us who intended to continue shaving our legs had the razors taken away. I thought they feared we'd slash our wrists on a bad day. Whatever the reason, all razors were confiscated on the first day. Helene was also older than most of us, having completed college before entering the convent. As a college graduate, she was expected to be more mature and responsible than the rest of us. The song she composed for the Christmas talent show dashed those expectations in the eyes of the Superior, but in our eyes, Helene got first prize. The song was set to the tune of "Let it Snow," but was entitled, "Let it Grow." It went like this:

> Oh, the hair on our legs is frightful,
> and a razor would be delightful,
> but since it doesn't show
> Let it grow! Let it grow! Let it grow!

Years later I read something by Anna Freud that said, "Creative minds have always been known to survive any kind of bad training," and Helene Moynihan was the first person to come to mind. And ever since, not a Christmas day goes by that I don't find myself singing a round of "Let it Grow" for friends and family, and telling the story of my first Christmas talent show in the convent when Helene Moynihan not only improved the social spirit of the community, but also made all around her very happy.

SHRIMP SCAMPI

Serves 4

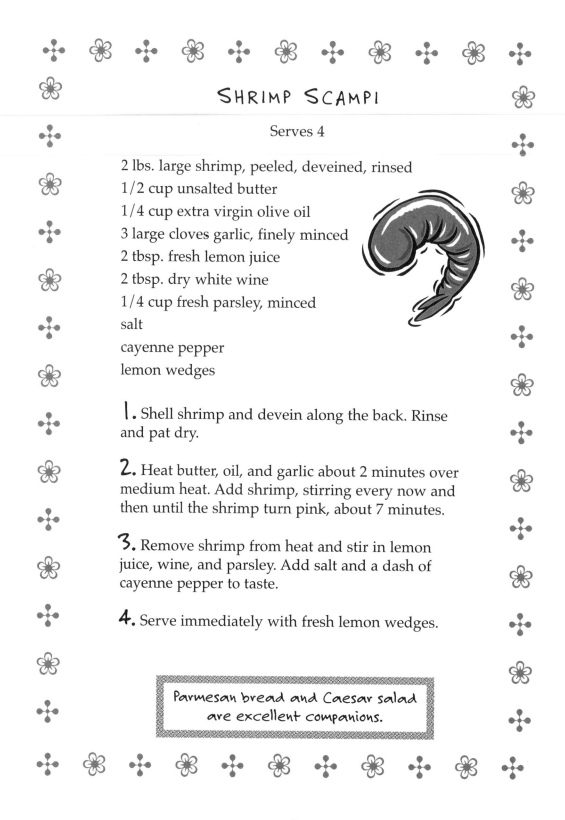

2 lbs. large shrimp, peeled, deveined, rinsed
1/2 cup unsalted butter
1/4 cup extra virgin olive oil
3 large cloves garlic, finely minced
2 tbsp. fresh lemon juice
2 tbsp. dry white wine
1/4 cup fresh parsley, minced
salt
cayenne pepper
lemon wedges

1. Shell shrimp and devein along the back. Rinse and pat dry.

2. Heat butter, oil, and garlic about 2 minutes over medium heat. Add shrimp, stirring every now and then until the shrimp turn pink, about 7 minutes.

3. Remove shrimp from heat and stir in lemon juice, wine, and parsley. Add salt and a dash of cayenne pepper to taste.

4. Serve immediately with fresh lemon wedges.

> Parmesan bread and Caesar salad
> are excellent companions.

DADDY'S BBQ RIBS

4 lbs. pork spareribs or one slab, cut into 3 rib pieces

salt and pepper to taste

1 large onion, coarsely chopped

1 cup brown sugar

3/4 cup chili sauce

1/4 cup soy sauce

1/4 cup Worcestershire sauce

1/4 cup dark rum

1 tsp. dry mustard

1/8 tsp. cayenne pepper

1 tsp. red pepper flakes

4 cloves garlic, crushed

1 small onion, chopped fine

1. Season ribs with salt and pepper, scatter coarsely chopped onion on top, wrap ribs in double thickness of foil, and bake at 350° for 1 1/2 hours.

2. To make the BBQ sauce, combine the remaining ingredients.

3. When the ribs are done baking, drain the drippings and pour BBQ sauce over each, saving some for basting. Cover and marinate in the refrigerator for 2 hours.

4. When ready, bake at 350° for 1/2 hour, or better yet, grill over hot coals for 1/2 hour. These can also be made the day before and left in the refrigerator overnight.

> The recipe that made these ribs famous.

MINNESOTA POT ROAST WITH DARK BEER

2 lb. beef roast (any kind works well, including the old standby chuck roast)

2 tbsp. olive oil

1 large onion, coarsely chopped

2 celery stalks, coarsely chopped

3 or 4 potatoes, peeled and cut into large chunks

1 lb. carrots, sliced thick

2 cups beef stock

1-12 oz. dark beer (NO LIGHT BEER)

2 bay leaves

3 tbsp. fresh thyme

1 tsp. brown sugar

2 tbsp. Dijon or whole-grain mustard

1 tbsp. tomato paste

salt and freshly ground pepper to taste

1. Preheat oven to 350°. Heat the oil in a large Dutch oven, then brown the meat on all sides.

2. Remove meat and drain on paper towels. Add onion to the pan and cook about 5 minutes or until it begins to brown.

3. Add celery, potato, and carrots to the pan and stir, cooking until they begin to brown. Then stir in the flour for about 1 minute, mixing everything well.

4. Pour in the beef stock and dark beer, mixing well, and bringing everything to a boil. Blend in the bay leaves, thyme, sugar, mustard, tomato paste, salt, and pepper.

5. Place the meat on top of everything, cover tightly, and roast in the oven for 2 1/2 hours.

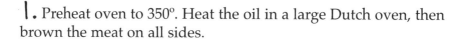

This makes its own gravy, and you'll want it every weekend.

CRANBERRY GLAZED PORK ROAST

4 lb. boneless pork loin roast
2 tbsp. cornstarch
1/4 tsp. cinnamon
1/8 tsp. salt
1/2 tsp. grated orange peel
2 tbsp. fresh orange juice
2 tbsp. dry sherry
1-10 oz. can whole berry cranberry sauce

1. Preheat oven to 325°. Put pork loin into a shallow baking dish and roast at 325° for 45 minutes.

2. Mix all other ingredients in a saucepan over medium heat until the sauce thickens. Set aside.

3. Remove roast from oven after 45 minutes and spoon 1/2 cup of sauce over the top and sides. Return roast to oven and bake 30 minutes more.

4. Let stand 10 minutes before slicing. Serve with the rest of the sauce.

QUICK AND EASY CHICKEN CACCIATORE

1-32 oz. can Italian plum tomatoes, crushed or whole, with basil

2 packets powdered Italian dressing mix

1 bay leaf

2 garlic cloves, minced

olive oil

1 onion, chopped fine

1 green pepper, chopped (optional)

1/2 lb. mushrooms, sliced

salt and freshly ground pepper

10 pieces of chicken

white wine

pasta of your choice

freshly grated Parmesan cheese

garlic bread

1. In a large saucepan, add tomatoes and powdered dressing mix, and simmer on medium heat. Add bay leaf and minced garlic.

2. Heat 3 tbsp. olive oil in a skillet and sauté onion and green pepper until soft. Add to tomato sauce and stir. Then sauté the mushrooms in the same skillet and add to the sauce as well.

3. Salt and pepper the chicken and sauté each piece in the skillet until lightly browned, adding more olive oil as necessary. While sautéing chicken, add a little white wine to the skillet. Remove browned chicken from skillet and add to tomato sauce, stirring well.

4. When all the chicken is added to the sauce, stir well, cover partially, and simmer on medium heat for 1 hour. Uncover and stir about every 10 to 15 minutes. Season to taste.

5. After about an hour, when the chicken begins to fall off the bone, serve over pasta with freshly grated Parmesan cheese and garlic bread to mop up the sauce.

> This is even better the next day.

82

Bolognese Pasta Sauce

Serves 4

3 tbsp. bacon, chopped
3 tbsp. unsalted butter
4 tbsp. prosciutto, chopped
2 small onions, finely chopped
2 carrots, finely chopped
2 celery stalks, finely chopped
1/2 lb. ground beef
1/2 lb. ground veal
1/4 lb. ground pork
1 cup chicken broth

1 cup dry white wine
1 lb. plum tomatoes, quartered
1 tsp. salt
2 tsp. freshly ground pepper
1 tsp. clove
1/3 tsp. ground nutmeg
2 cups hot water (if needed)
1/2 lb. mushrooms, sliced
3/4 cup heavy cream
pasta, your choice

1. In a large saucepan, sauté bacon in butter until soft, then add prosciutto and simmer for 2 minutes. Add onions, carrots, and celery, and cook until soft.

2. Mix ground beef, veal, and pork and add to saucepan, simmering until meat is lightly browned and half cooked.

3. Add the chicken broth and white wine, stirring constantly until sauce thickens.

4. Add the tomatoes, salt, pepper, clove, and nutmeg and blend well. If the sauce is too thick, add a little hot water. Cover and simmer over low heat for 1 hour, stirring frequently.

5. Raise the heat, add the mushrooms, and cook uncovered 5 minutes more.

6. Just before serving, blend in the cream. Serve over the pasta of your choice.

GOOD OLD MEATLOAF

Serves 4

1 tbsp. olive oil
3/4 cup onion, finely chopped
3 large eggs
1 1/2 lbs. ground chuck
1/2 cup seasoned (or not) bread crumbs
1/2 cup ketchup
1 tbsp. steak sauce
1 tsp. freshly ground pepper
1 tsp. salt
1 tsp. garlic, minced

1. Heat oil in skillet and sauté onions until tender, about 5 minutes. Remove and cool.

2. In a large bowl, whisk eggs until blended, then add onion and rest of ingredients. Mix with hands until well blended, but don't over mix.

3. Grease a baking sheet (with sides); form the meat mixture into a loaf, and bake at 350° for one hour.

Great with garlic mashed potatoes.

Louisiana Shrimp Creole

Makes 6–8 servings

6 tbsp. butter

1 1/2 cup onion, coarsely chopped

4 ribs celery, coarsely chopped

1 green pepper, coarsely chopped

6 cloves garlic, minced

4 cups canned plum tomatoes

4 sprigs fresh thyme, or 1 tsp. dried

2 bay leaves

Tabasco sauce, to taste

1 tsp. grated lemon rind

salt and pepper, to taste

2 lbs. fresh large shrimp, shelled, deveined, rinsed, patted dry

4 tbsp. fresh parsley, chopped

juice of one lemon

rice

1. In a large saucepan, melt butter and sauté onion until wilted. Add celery, green pepper, and garlic, sautéing briefly, keeping the veggies crisp.

2. Add tomatoes, thyme, bay leaves, Tabasco, lemon rind, salt, and pepper, and simmer uncovered for 10–15 minutes.

3. Add shrimp, stir well, cover, and cook for 3–5 minutes. Right before serving add parsley and lemon juice. Serve over rice.

PIGS IN A BLANKET

1 head green cabbage
2 lbs. ground chuck
1 cup cooked white rice
1 cup onion, finely chopped
salt and pepper to taste
1 can tomato soup
1 soup can water
6 bacon strips

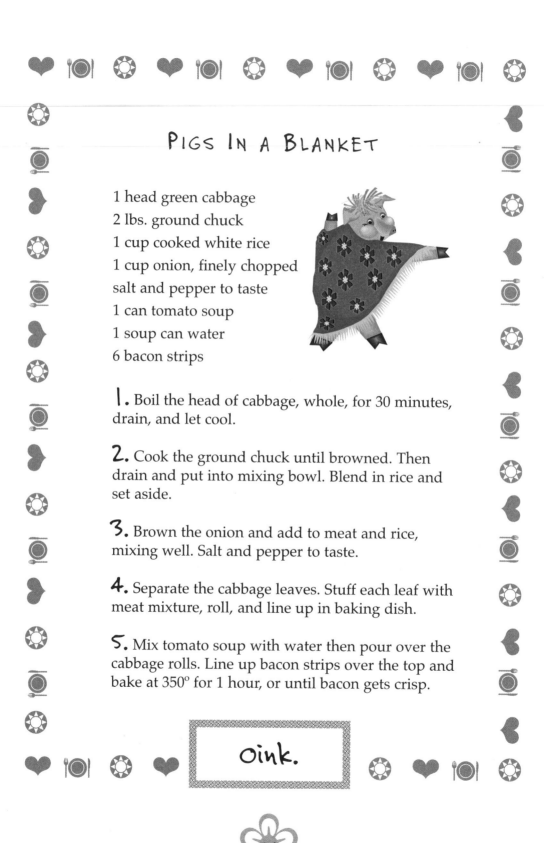

1. Boil the head of cabbage, whole, for 30 minutes, drain, and let cool.

2. Cook the ground chuck until browned. Then drain and put into mixing bowl. Blend in rice and set aside.

3. Brown the onion and add to meat and rice, mixing well. Salt and pepper to taste.

4. Separate the cabbage leaves. Stuff each leaf with meat mixture, roll, and line up in baking dish.

5. Mix tomato soup with water then pour over the cabbage rolls. Line up bacon strips over the top and bake at 350° for 1 hour, or until bacon gets crisp.

Oink.

PORK CHOPS AND SCALLOPED POTATOES

Serves 6

2 cups half and half
2 cloves garlic, sliced thin
4 tbsp. Dijon mustard
2 tsp. dried thyme
3 cups potatoes, thinly sliced
2 tbsp. unsalted butter
6 pork chops, loin cut
1/4 cup dry white wine
1 cup onion, thinly sliced
2 tbsp. fresh parsley, finely chopped
1/2 tsp. freshly ground pepper

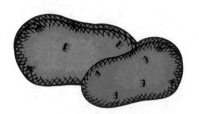

1. Add half and half and garlic to a large saucepan and bring to a boil. Lower the heat and simmer 8–10 minutes, until it's reduced by a third. Then remove from heat, add mustard and thyme, mix well, and set aside.

2. Fill a large saucepan with water and bring to a boil. Add potato slices and cook for about 30 seconds. Then drain, rinse with cold water, and dry on paper towel.

3. In a skillet, melt butter and brown pork chops over medium-high heat for about 2–3 minutes on each side. Turn only once. The more you turn the meat, the tougher it gets. Remove the chops when done and set aside. Then add the wine to the skillet and mix with buttered remnants for about 30 seconds.

4. In an 8"x12" baking dish, layer half the potatoes and onions. Then lay the pork chops on top and pour the skillet juices over all. Top with the rest of the potatoes and onions and pour the cream mixture on top. Scatter parsley on top with pepper. Bake at 350° for 1 hour and 15 minutes, then pop under the broiler for a few minutes, browning the top.

Divine Sides

Honey-Glazed Acorn Squash

Serves 4

2 acorn squash
6 tbsp. unsalted butter, melted
1/3 cup honey
1 tbsp. brown sugar
1/2 tsp. salt
1/4 tsp. ground cinnamon
1/4 tsp. ground ginger

1. Cut squash in half, clean, and place in a shallow baking pan, cut side down. Add 1/2-inch water. Bake 30 minutes in oven at 375°.

2. Remove a small slice from bottom of each squash half so they will stay level while baking.

3. Combine the butter, honey, brown sugar, salt, cinnamon, and ginger and mix well. Spoon the mixture into center of squash.

4. Return to oven and bake 15-20 minutes more until tender.

SMOTHERED CABBAGE

Makes 4-6 servings

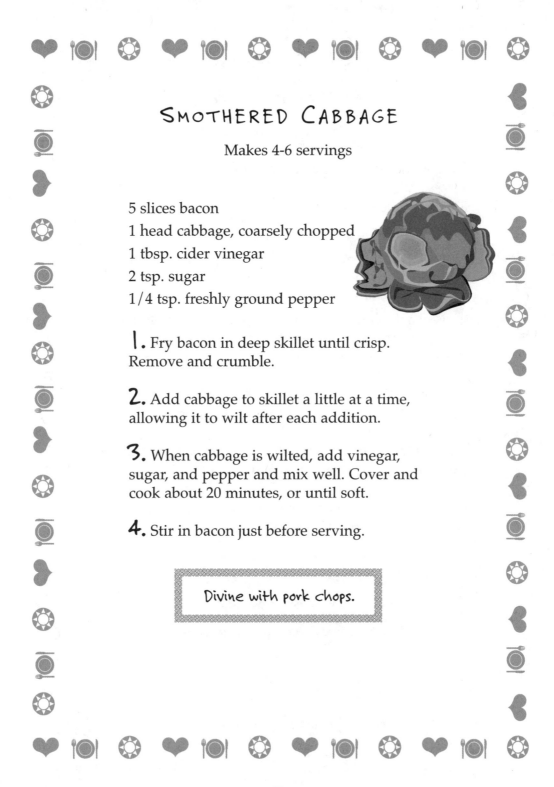

5 slices bacon
1 head cabbage, coarsely chopped
1 tbsp. cider vinegar
2 tsp. sugar
1/4 tsp. freshly ground pepper

1. Fry bacon in deep skillet until crisp. Remove and crumble.

2. Add cabbage to skillet a little at a time, allowing it to wilt after each addition.

3. When cabbage is wilted, add vinegar, sugar, and pepper and mix well. Cover and cook about 20 minutes, or until soft.

4. Stir in bacon just before serving.

> Divine with pork chops.

SAL'S GARLIC MASHED POTATOES

Makes 4 servings

5 big Idaho potatoes (never use anything other than
   Idahos)
8 large whole cloves garlic, peeled
1/2 cup butter
1/2 cup half and half
salt to taste

1. Peel and chop the potatoes into cubes. Add to pan with just enough water to cover the potatoes. Too much water kills the potato.

2. Throw the garlic cloves into the water with the potatoes. Don't be afraid of too much garlic.

3. Turn the heat on high and cook until potatoes are soft. Then remove from heat and drain.

4. Mash potatoes with garlic, adding the butter, cream, and salt to taste.

These are the best.

Good Old Green Bean Casserole

Serves 6

1 can cream of mushroom soup

1/2 cup milk

1 tsp. soy sauce

pepper, to taste

4 cups fresh green beans, cooked (or two packs frozen green beans)

1-6 oz. can French-fried onions

1. In a 1 1/2 qt. casserole dish, stir soup, milk, soy sauce, and pepper until smooth.

2. Mix in beans and 1/2 cup onions.

3. Bake at 350° for 25 minutes, then remove, stir, top with remaining onions, and bake 5 minutes more.

SWEET POTATO CASSEROLE

Serves 6–8

6 large sweet potatoes
1/4 cup butter, softened
1/2 cup half and half
1/2 cup red wine
1/2 tsp. salt
1/2 tsp. ground cinnamon
1/2 tsp. ground nutmeg
1/4 cup sugar
freshly ground pepper, to taste
butter, as needed
brown sugar
chopped pecans

1. Preheat oven to 375° and bake potatoes until tender, about 30-40 minutes.

2. Remove potatoes and lower oven temperature to 350°. Peel and mash potatoes, adding butter, half and half, and wine. Blend well, then add salt, cinnamon, nutmeg, sugar, and pepper to taste.

3. Butter an 8-cup casserole dish and put in sweet potato mix. Dot with butter and sprinkle with brown sugar and chopped pecans. Bake at 350° for 30 minutes.

MAPLE-ROASTED BABY CARROTS

Serves 6–8

2-16 oz. bags baby carrots
2 tbsp. olive oil
1/2 tsp. salt
4 tbsp. butter
4 tbsp. maple syrup

1. Preheat oven to 475°. Toss carrots with oil and salt, spread a single layer in a baking pan, and roast for 12 minutes, shaking the pan to toss the carrots so they roast evenly.

2. In a small saucepan, melt butter, and simmer until it begins to brown, about 1–2 minutes. Remove from heat and stir in maple syrup.

3. After 12 minutes of roasting, drizzle the butter and maple syrup over the carrots, shaking the pan to coat the carrots well. Return the pan to the oven and roast 8 minutes more, shaking a couple of times more until the carrots are tender and begin to brown.

> Even if you hate carrots, you'll love these.

SAUSAGE STUFFING

Serves 6

8 slices stale white bread, toasted lightly and cut
   into cubes, or 1 bag bread cubes, unseasoned

1 lb. bulk breakfast sausage

1/4 cup butter, melted

3/4 cup celery, finely chopped

3/4 cup onion, finely chopped

1 egg

1/2 cup parsley, coarsely chopped

1 tsp. poultry seasoning

1/2 cup chicken bouillon/stock

salt and pepper

1. Put bread cubes in a big bowl. Brown sausage in skillet, drain fat, and mix in with bread cubes.

2. Sauté butter, celery, and onion lightly in same skillet, then mix with bread and sausage.

3. Beat egg lightly and mix into bread. Blend in parsley and poultry seasoning. Add bouillon a little at a time to moisten well. Salt and pepper to taste.

4. Bake in casserole dish at 350° for 1 hour, or until golden brown.

> This recipe makes enough for a 14 lb. turkey,
> or makes an excellent side dish with chicken and pork.

SAL'S SAUTÉED SPINACH AND GARLIC

Makes 4 servings

5 tbsp. olive oil
5 large garlic cloves, peeled and sliced paper-thin
1 big bag of spinach, washed and dried
salt, to taste

1. Heat olive oil in a deep frying pan, and sauté garlic until soft, but not brown.

2. Add spinach to pan, stir, and cover while spinach cooks down. About every 5 minutes, uncover to stir, and keep stirring until spinach is cooked to your liking. Salt to taste.

This is a basic food group for Sally Davies: vegetarian, artist, and best friend.

TWICE-BAKED POTATOES

Serves 8

4 Yukon Gold potatoes

1 cup sharp cheddar cheese (or cheese of your choice)

1/2 cup buttermilk

1/2 cup sour cream

2 tbsp. unsalted butter, softened

1/2 cup scallions, sliced thin (white and green part)

1/2 tsp. salt

8 slices bacon, fried crisp and crumbled

freshly ground pepper, to taste

1. Preheat oven to 400°. Scrub, dry, and rub potatoes with vegetable oil. Bake on foil-lined pan about 1 hour, or until skin is crisp. Remove and let potatoes sit 15 minutes or so, until they're cool enough to handle.

2. Cut the potato in half, and scoop out the insides, leaving about 1/8 inch of potato in each skin. Return the scooped out skins to the oven, and bake another 10 minutes, until crisped.

3. Mash the potatoes with the remaining ingredients, blending well. Scoop the mix into the crisped skins, increase oven to 500°, and broil until brown and crispy on top, about 10 minutes more. Allow to cool a bit before serving.

HARVARD BEETS

Serves 4–6, depending on who likes beets

2 lbs. beets, cleaned
1/2 cup sugar
5 tbsp. red wine vinegar
2 tsp. cornstarch
1/3 cup freshly squeezed orange juice
salt and freshly ground pepper, to taste
1 tbsp. unsalted butter

1. In a medium saucepan, cover the beets with water and bring to a boil. Reduce heat to low, cover, and cook beets until tender, about 45 minutes. Drain and rinse under cold water. Remove the skins, and slice beets into a bowl.

2. In a heavy saucepan over medium heat, add sugar, vinegar, cornstarch, orange juice, salt, and pepper, whisking constantly until the mixture boils and thickens, about 5 minutes. Then whisk in the butter and cook until it melts.

3. Pour the sauce over the beets and toss. These can be served hot or at room temperature.

> I could eat the whole thing.

97

Just Desserts

"To preserve and increase the spirit of union, the sisters shall in all circumstances show mutual esteem and loyalty. They shall love one another sincerely, never entertaining feelings of aversion."
—Constitution #215

"The monotony of a quiet life stimulates the creative mind."
—Albert Einstein

Loving one another sincerely without entertaining feelings of aversion is just as impossible in the sisterhood as it is anywhere else. It often seems like some people just ask for it; they are so irritating that we cannot help but entertain feelings of aversion. Because we spent so much of our day in the convent in silence, there wasn't much time to entertain any feelings, including those of aversion. But that didn't prevent some of us from entertaining such uncharitable feelings anyway.

For some of us, the sisters who invited the strongest feelings of aversion were those who demonstrated an insatiable desire for obedience. They loved being told what to do and relished every opportunity to dismiss their practical judgment and conform to the will of the Superior. While the rest of us were miserable, they were smiling and happy. When we complained, they complied. They never entertained feelings of aversion about anyone or anything. They were called the "living rule." They lived the rule of the sisterhood to the letter, and did so with joyful hearts and smiling eyes. While I was once told by the Mother Superior that I "smiled with my teeth but not my eyes," the truly obedient smiled with both.

There were several "living rules" in our class that shot the curve for the rest of us, and my best friend Mary Ann Pajakowski wrote a poem that summed up the feelings of aversion many of us entertained. It's called "The Sunbeam."

The Sunbeam
She was a sunbeam,
All sparkling and bright,
Shedding her rays
From left and from right.
She was a sunbeam
With zeal unabated.
She was a sunbeam
And boy was she hated.

Karol and her mom, 1967.

The monotony of the quiet life did nothing but stimulate Paj's creative mind. She also wrote a one-act play for Thanksgiving called "The Ugly Pilgrim Girl." It was about a young girl who was so ugly the pilgrims thought she was a turkey and shot her. I suppose you'd call that a severe case of entertaining feelings of aversion, which is probably why the Constitutions ruled against it. But Paj is still a Sister of the Holy Cross after all these years, which just goes to show you that entertaining feelings of aversion can be also be a saving grace. None of the "sunbeams" we knew lasted.

left to right: dad, Karol, and grandpa, 1967.

Karol with her 2 brothers on the right and their friend (on the left), 1967.

Extra Creamy Cheesecake

Crust

1 1/2 cups graham cracker crumbs

1/3 cup brown sugar

1/2 tsp. ground cinnamon

1/4 cup unsalted butter (softened)

Butter the bottom of a 10-inch springform pan. Mix crumbs, sugar, cinnamon, and butter well. Press evenly into bottom of pan, and bake at 350° for 10 minutes. Set aside.

Filling

4-8 oz. packages cream cheese

1 cup sugar

5 eggs

2 1/2 tsp. vanilla extract

3 tbsp. flour

Cream the cheese and sugar first, then beat in eggs, one at a time. Add vanilla and flour; mix well. Pour into pan and bake at 350° for 1 1/2 hours. When done, remove and turn the oven up to 500°.

Topping

1 1/2 cup sour cream

1 tsp. vanilla extract

1/2 cup sugar

Mix sour cream, vanilla, and sugar well. Spread on top of cheesecake. Bake at 500° for 5 minutes. Cool, chill, and serve plain or with fresh berries.

BLESSED BANANA CREAM PIE

3 tbsp. cornstarch
1/4 tsp. salt
1 2/3 cups water
1-14 oz. can sweetened condensed milk
3 large egg yolks, beaten
2 tbsp. unsalted butter
1 1/2 tsp. vanilla extract
3 medium bananas
1/4 cup fresh lemon juice
1-9 inch pie shell, baked

1. In a medium-sized saucepan, and over medium heat, dissolve cornstarch, salt, and water. Then stir in milk and egg yolks; keep stirring until thick and bubbly. Remove from heat. Add butter and vanilla and mix well. Let cool.

2. Slice two of the bananas. Dip each slice in lemon juice, then arrange them on the bottom and sides of baked pie shell. Pour the filling over the bananas, cover with plastic wrap, and refrigerate at least 4 hours.

3. When ready to serve, slice remaining banana, dip slices in lemon juice, and arrange them on top of pie. Serve with fresh whipped cream. Refrigerate leftovers, if there are any.

COCONUT CUSTARD PIE

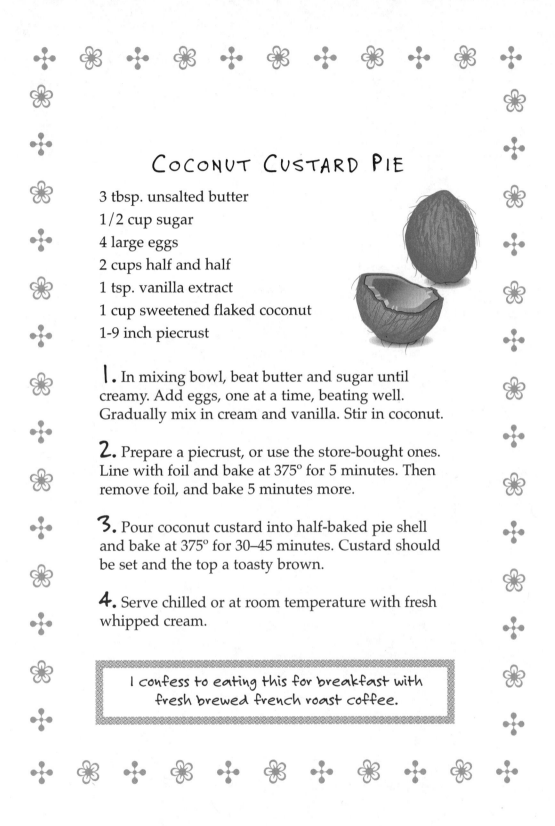

3 tbsp. unsalted butter
1/2 cup sugar
4 large eggs
2 cups half and half
1 tsp. vanilla extract
1 cup sweetened flaked coconut
1-9 inch piecrust

1. In mixing bowl, beat butter and sugar until creamy. Add eggs, one at a time, beating well. Gradually mix in cream and vanilla. Stir in coconut.

2. Prepare a piecrust, or use the store-bought ones. Line with foil and bake at 375° for 5 minutes. Then remove foil, and bake 5 minutes more.

3. Pour coconut custard into half-baked pie shell and bake at 375° for 30–45 minutes. Custard should be set and the top a toasty brown.

4. Serve chilled or at room temperature with fresh whipped cream.

> I confess to eating this for breakfast with fresh brewed french roast coffee.

KEY LIME PIE

4 tsp. grated lime zest

4 large egg yolks

1-14 oz. can sweetened condensed milk

1/2 cup fresh, strained lime juice from about 4 to 6 limes (key limes if available)

graham cracker crust (prepared)

whipped cream

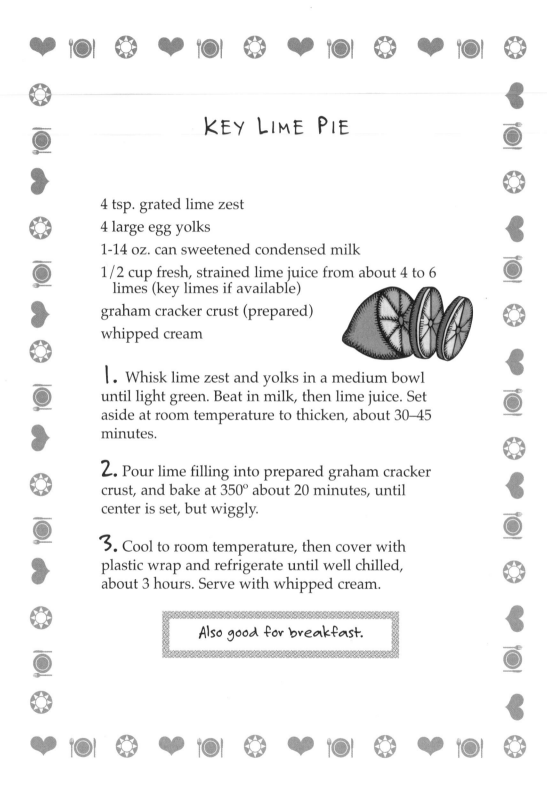

1. Whisk lime zest and yolks in a medium bowl until light green. Beat in milk, then lime juice. Set aside at room temperature to thicken, about 30–45 minutes.

2. Pour lime filling into prepared graham cracker crust, and bake at 350° about 20 minutes, until center is set, but wiggly.

3. Cool to room temperature, then cover with plastic wrap and refrigerate until well chilled, about 3 hours. Serve with whipped cream.

Also good for breakfast.

PUMPKIN PIE

3 large eggs
1/4 cup white sugar
1/3 cup brown sugar
2 cups canned pumpkin (unseasoned)
1 tsp. ground ginger
1 1/2 tsp. ground cinnamon
1/2 tsp. ground allspice
3/4 cup heavy cream
3/4 cup half and half
1-9 inch piecrust
whipped cream

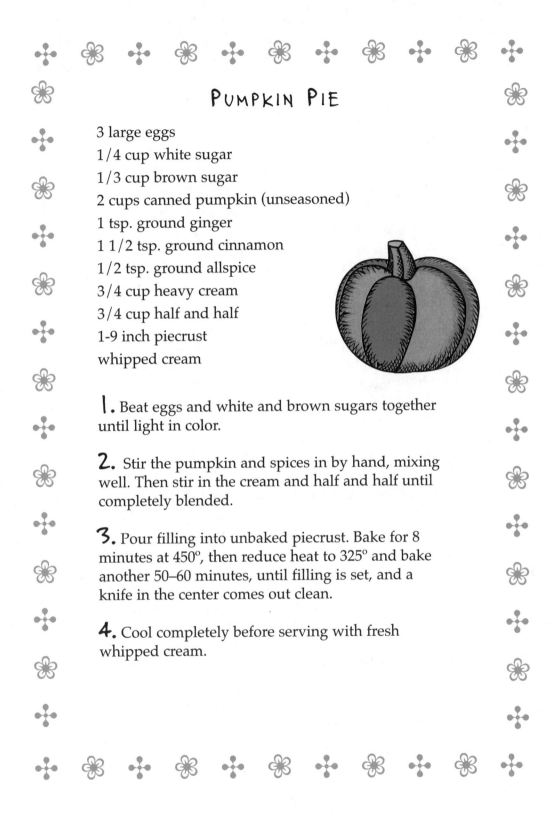

1. Beat eggs and white and brown sugars together until light in color.

2. Stir the pumpkin and spices in by hand, mixing well. Then stir in the cream and half and half until completely blended.

3. Pour filling into unbaked piecrust. Bake for 8 minutes at 450°, then reduce heat to 325° and bake another 50–60 minutes, until filling is set, and a knife in the center comes out clean.

4. Cool completely before serving with fresh whipped cream.

CRÈME BRULEE

3 whole eggs
3 egg yolks
2 1/2 cups heavy cream
1/2 cup milk
1/4 cup sugar

1 1/2 tsp. vanilla extract
dash of fresh nutmeg
1 cup brown sugar
6 custard cups

1. Beat the eggs and egg yolks together well and set aside.

2. In a saucepan, add cream, milk, and sugar. Heat at medium until the mixture begins to boil, then remove from heat. Slowly whisk the cream mixture with the eggs until well blended. Pour back into saucepan, and cook over medium heat about 5 minutes, or until it reaches the consistency of custard. Remove from heat, and stir in vanilla and nutmeg.

3. Pour custard into cups and place in 9"x13" baking pan. Pour boiling water into the pan making it level with the custard in the cups (*not* the top of the cups).

4. Bake at 350° for 45 minutes, or until custard is set. Then remove and cool. When cool, cover and chill for at least 6 hours, or overnight.

5. Several hours before serving, sift brown sugar on top of custard, and pop under the broiler for 1–2 minutes, until the sugar caramelizes. Remove and chill again before serving.

BUTTERSCOTCH PUDDING

Serves 6–8

2 cups milk
2 cups half and half
2 tbsp. unsalted butter
1 1/2 cups dark brown sugar, firmly packed
3 tbsp. cornstarch
1/2 tsp. salt
4 large eggs
1 tbsp. real vanilla extract
whipped cream

1. In a bowl, mix together milk and half and half. Set aside.

2. In a medium saucepan over low heat, melt the butter with sugar, then crank up the heat to high and bring to a boil, stirring constantly. Lower the heat to medium, add 3 cups of milk/cream blend and cook about 5 minutes, until mixture begins to thicken.

3. In a small bowl, make a paste with the cornstarch and a little of the milk/cream. Stir the paste into the rest of the milk/cream and add to the pan. Cook over medium heat for about 10 minutes, until it thickens, then stir in the salt. Remove from heat.

4. Beat the eggs lightly, just to blend, then pour a little of the mixture from the pan in with the eggs, stirring until well blended. Whisk the egg mix into the pan, return to heat, and stir constantly until it comes to a boil, about 5 minutes. Then remove the pan from heat and stir in the vanilla.

5. Spoon into pudding bowls, chill, and serve with fresh whipped cream.

CREAMY DREAMY
RICE PUDDING

1/2 cup white rice
1 cup milk
1 cup heavy cream
1 tsp. vanilla extract
7 tbsp. sugar
1 1/2 tsp. ground cinnamon
1/8 tsp. fresh ground nutmeg

1. Cook the rice as directed, until most of the water is absorbed.

2. Mix in the milk, cream, vanilla, and sugar. Bring to a boil, then simmer about 1 hour and 15 minutes, until it reaches the consistency you like. Stir every 10 to 15 minutes.

3. Remove from heat and mix in cinnamon and nutmeg, or sprinkle them on top when serving warm or chilled.

> The ultimate comfort food.

BREAD PUDDING WITH WHISKEY SAUCE

Pudding

1 loaf (16 slices) stale French or
  Italian bread

2 cups half and half

2 cups milk

3 eggs

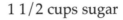

1 1/2 cups sugar

1/4 tsp. nutmeg

2 tsp. vanilla extract

1/2 cup raisins

1. Break bread into bowl, cover with half and half and milk. Set aside.

2. In a separate bowl, beat together eggs, sugar, nutmeg, and vanilla. Then add this to the bread mixture and stir well. Add raisins and mix again.

3. Grease a 9"x13" baking pan. Pour bread mix into pan and bake at 325° on the middle rack of the oven for 1 hour and 15 minutes. The top should be browned and the custard set. Remove and cool.

Sauce

1/2 cup unsalted butter, softened

1 1/2 cups powdered sugar

1 egg

4 tbsp. whiskey or brandy

1. In the top of a double boiler, stir together butter and powdered sugar. When the sugar dissolves and the sauce is hot, but not boiling, remove from heat.

2. Beat the egg well and whisk it in with the butter and sugar. Continue whisking until the sauce begins to cool. Then add whiskey or brandy to taste.

Cut the pudding into squares, top with sauce, and serve.

MABLE'S PINEAPPLE DELITE

2 1/2 cups graham cracker crumbs
1 cup unsalted butter, softened
1 1/2 cups powdered sugar
2 large unbeaten eggs
1-14 oz. can crushed pineapple, drained well
1 cup of whipping cream, whipped

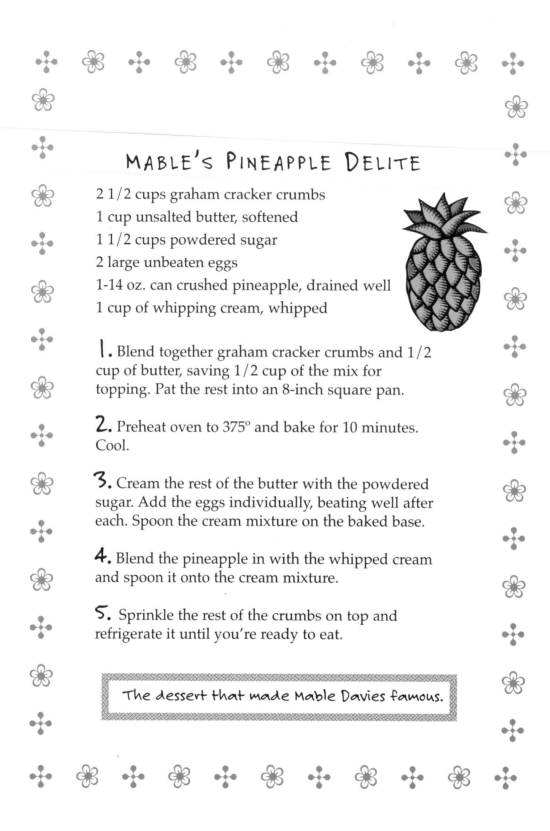

1. Blend together graham cracker crumbs and 1/2 cup of butter, saving 1/2 cup of the mix for topping. Pat the rest into an 8-inch square pan.

2. Preheat oven to 375° and bake for 10 minutes. Cool.

3. Cream the rest of the butter with the powdered sugar. Add the eggs individually, beating well after each. Spoon the cream mixture on the baked base.

4. Blend the pineapple in with the whipped cream and spoon it onto the cream mixture.

5. Sprinkle the rest of the crumbs on top and refrigerate it until you're ready to eat.

The dessert that made Mable Davies famous.

KATE'S PEACH AND RASPBERRY COBBLER

1 cup flour
1 tbsp. baking powder
1 cup sugar
1/2 tsp. salt
1 egg
1 cup milk
1/2 cup unsalted better
2 cups fresh peaches, skinned and sliced
1/2 cup fresh raspberries

1. In a medium-sized bowl, blend the flour, baking powder, sugar, and salt.

2. Mix the egg and milk in a separate bowl.

3. Melt butter in an 8-inch square pan.

4. Mix the wet and dry ingredients together and pour into the pan with melted butter.

5. Add the peaches and raspberries and let fruit settle.

6. Bake at 400° for 40 minutes.

Serve hot with vanilla ice cream. Yummers.

PINEAPPLE UPSIDE-DOWN CAKE

Topping

1/4 cup unsalted butter, softened

1/2 cup dark brown sugar

1-8 oz. can crushed pineapple, drained (save 2 tbsp. juice for cake)

Cake

1 cup flour

3/4 cup sugar

1 tsp. baking powder

1/4 tsp. salt

1 egg

1/2 cup milk

1/3 cup unsalted butter, softened

2 tbsp. pineapple juice

1. Preheat oven to 350°. In a 9-inch round cake pan, blend the butter and sugar, then place in the oven until the mixture begins to melt. Remove, add pineapple, mix well, and spread the mixture to make an even layer of topping in the bottom of the pan.

2. In a mixing bowl, combine all the cake ingredients and mix at a low speed until well blended. Pour over pineapple mixture, and bake at 350° for 35–40 minutes.

3. Remove from oven and invert onto a serving plate. Serve warm or at room temperature with fresh whipped cream.

RED DEVIL CAKE

Serves 12

Cake

1 cup unsalted butter	2 1/2 cups all purpose flour
2 cups sugar	1 tbsp. white vinegar
3 large eggs	1 1/2 tsp. baking soda
1 cup buttermilk	1/2 tsp. salt
6 oz. grated semi-sweet chocolate	1 tsp. vanilla extract
	2 oz. red food coloring

Frosting

1/2 cup unsalted butter, softened

12 oz. cream cheese (a brick and a half), softened

3 cups powdered sugar

2 tsp. vanilla extract

1 cup chopped pecans (optional)

1. In a large bowl, cream butter and sugar. Add eggs and beat until fluffy. Whisk in buttermilk, chocolate, flour, vinegar, soda, and salt; then whisk in vanilla and food coloring.

2. Pour into a greased 9"x13" pan or three greased 8-inch round cake pans. Bake at 325° for 35–40 minutes or until a toothpick inserted in the center comes out clean. Let cakes cool in pan about 10 minutes before inverting onto racks to cool before frosting.

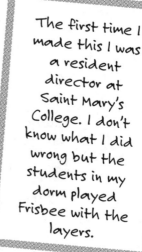

The first time I made this I was a resident director at Saint Mary's College. I don't know what I did wrong but the students in my dorm played Frisbee with the layers.

3. In a large bowl, beat the butter and cream cheese until smooth. Then lower speed and blend in powdered sugar and vanilla. When everything is well blended, turn speed up to medium high and beat until fluffy, about 2–3 minutes. Add pecans at this point, if you want to.

4. Frost the cake and chill before serving.

CHOCOLATE CAKE WITH MILK CHOCOLATE FROSTING

Cake

1 1/2 cups flour

1/2 cup unsweetened cocoa, preferably Dutch process

1/4 tsp. baking powder

1/2 tsp. baking soda

salt, dash

3/4 cup unsalted butter, softened

1 cup sugar

1/2 cup brown sugar

2 large eggs

2 tsp. vanilla extract

1 cup buttermilk

Frosting

10 oz. milk chocolate, chopped

1/2 cup heavy cream

salt, dash

1 tbsp. light corn syrup

1/2 cup powdered sugar

1/2 cup unsalted butter, cold and cut into 8 pieces

1. Sift together flour, cocoa, baking powder, soda, and salt. Set aside.

2. In a mixing bowl, beat butter until creamy, then add sugar and beat 3–4 minutes, until light and fluffy. Beat in eggs, one at a time, then add vanilla and beat for 15 seconds.

3. On low speed, add dry ingredients alternately with buttermilk, and mix until smooth and velvety.

4. Grease and flour two 8-inch round cake pans. Pour batter evenly into pans, and bake on middle rack at 350° for 30 minutes. Let cool for 15 minutes before removing from pan.

5. Make frosting. Put chocolate chunks into a food processor and process until finely chopped.

6. Heat cream, salt, and corn syrup in a separate pan until the mixture begins to boil, then add to chocolate through feed tube, processing about 1 minute.

7. Stop the machine, add powdered sugar, and process to blend, about 30 seconds. Add butter one piece at a time, processing until smooth, another 20 or 30 seconds.

8. Pour frosting into a bowl and let cool at room temperature, stirring frequently until it thickens, about 1 hour.

9. Then frost cake and serve.

COCONUT CAKE

Serves 8

Cake

1 large egg

5 egg whites

1/4 cup water

3/4 cup cream of coconut

1 tsp. coconut extract

1 tsp. vanilla extract

2 1/4 cups cake flour, sifted

1 tbsp. baking powder

1 cup sugar

1/2 tsp. salt

3/4 cup unsalted butter, cut into 12 pieces

Frosting

4 large egg whites

1 cup sugar

a pinch of salt

2 cups unsalted butter, cut into 24 pieces

1/4 cup cream of coconut

1 tsp. vanilla extract

1 tsp. coconut extract

8 oz. sweetened coconut flakes

1. In a small bowl, beat egg and whites with a fork to combine, then add water, coconut cream, coconut extract and vanilla and blend well.

2. In a big mixing bowl, blend flour, baking powder, sugar, and salt. With a mixer on low speed add butter piece by piece until the dough looks coarse and mealy. Slowly add egg mixture and beat until fluffy. The batter will be thick.

3. Grease and flour 2 9-inch round cake pans and divide the batter between them. Bake at 325° for about 30 minutes. Cake should be golden brown and a toothpick inserted in the middle comes out clean. Cool for 10 minutes before inverting on a rack to cool completely before icing.

4. Over a saucepan of simmering hot water set a mixing bowl with egg whites, sugar, and a pinch of salt. Whisk about two minutes until the mixture becomes opaque and warm, then remove from heat and beat until egg whites are shiny and sticky, about 7–8 minutes. Reduce mixer speed to medium and beat in butter one piece at a time. Then add the coconut cream and extracts, beating until well combined.

5. Frost the cake, cover with coconut flakes, and refrigerate. Bring to room temperature before serving.

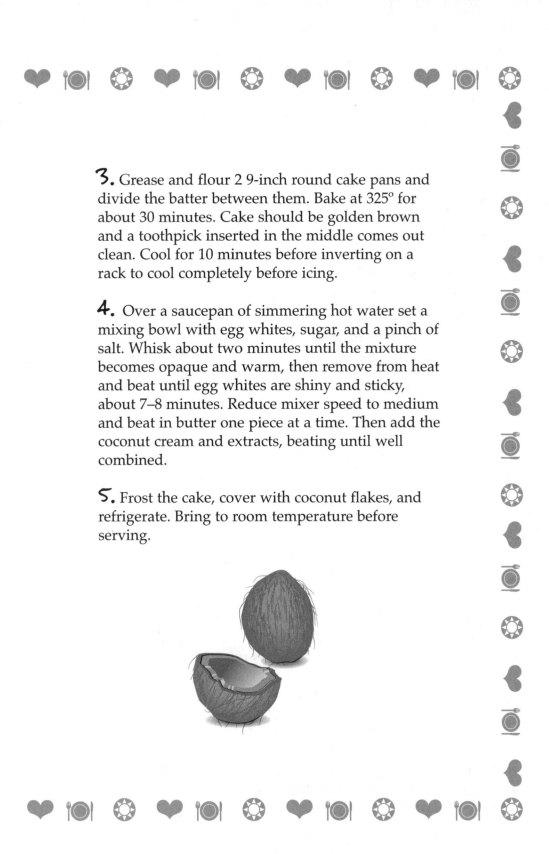

LEMON POPPYSEED POUNDCAKE

Cake

1 cup butter, softened

2 cups sugar

5 large eggs

2 cups flour

2 tsp. baking powder

1/2 cup buttermilk

1 tbsp. fresh lemon juice

1 tbsp. lemon rind, grated

1 tsp. vanilla extract

1/2 cup poppy seeds

Syrup

1/3 cup sugar

1/3 cup fresh lemon juice

1/3 cup water

3 tbsp. lemon rind, grated

1. Cream butter and sugar until light and fluffy. Add eggs one at a time, beating well.

2. Sift flour and baking powder into a separate bowl. Add dry ingredients alternately with buttermilk to batter and mix well. Then fold in lemon juice and rind, vanilla, and poppy seeds.

3. Grease and flour a loaf pan. Pour in the batter and bake for 1 hour at 350°, or until top springs back when touched. Cool 15 minutes before removing from pan.

4. Combine syrup ingredients in saucepan and bring to boil. While cake is still warm, brush the top and sides with syrup. Cut and serve.

THOSE REAL GOOD LEMON BARS

Makes about 36 squares, depending on size

2 1/4 cups flour

1/2 cup powdered sugar

1 cup unsalted butter, cold, cut into 12 pieces (no margarine allowed)

6 eggs, slightly beaten

3/4 cup fresh lemon juice (about 3 lemons)

1 1/2 tbsp. grated lemon peel

3 cups sugar

6 tbsp. flour

3/4 tsp. baking powder

powdered sugar

1. Preheat oven to 325° and grease a 15"x10" jelly roll pan.

2. In a food processor (or by hand with a pastry blender), combine flour, powdered sugar, and butter. Pulse or chop until the mixture resembles fine crumbs.

3. Press the crumb mixture evenly on the bottom and up the sides of the pan and bake for 15 minutes. Remove from oven and increase heat to 350°.

4. In a medium-sized bowl, beat the eggs slightly to blend, then add lemon juice and grated peel. In a separate bowl, combine sugar, 6 tbsp. flour, and baking powder. Stir into egg mixture.

5. Pour mixture over the crust and bake for 30 minutes, or until the center springs back when touched.

6. Sprinkle with powdered sugar, and when completely cool, cut into squares.

HERSHEY'S KISSES COOKIES

Makes about 3 dozen

1/2 cup sugar
1/2 cup brown sugar
1/2 cup shortening
1/2 cup creamy peanut butter
1 egg
1 tsp. vanilla extract
1 3/4 cups flour
1 tsp. baking soda
1/2 tsp. salt
Hershey's Kisses

1. Cream sugars, shortening, and peanut butter. Add egg and vanilla. Sift dry ingredients together in a separate bowl. Mix together wet and dry ingredients.

2. Roll teaspoons of dough into 1-inch balls, roll in sugar, flatten slightly, and place on a cookie sheet. Bake at 350° for about 10 minutes, then take out of oven and press a chocolate kiss in the center of each cookie. Return to the oven and bake for another 5 minutes.

THE $250 COOKIE RECIPE

Makes 10 dozen

2 cups butter
2 cups sugar
2 cups brown sugar
4 large eggs
2 tsp. vanilla extract
4 cups flour
5 cups oatmeal
1 tsp. salt
2 tsp. baking powder
2 tsp. baking soda
4 cups chocolate chips (2-12 oz. bags)
1-8 oz. chocolate bar, chunked
3 cups pecans, chopped

1. In a large bowl, mix together butter, sugar, and brown sugar. Add eggs and vanilla, mixing well.

2. In a separate bowl, combine flour, oatmeal, salt, baking powder and baking soda. Mix everything together, then add chocolates and pecans.

3. Preheat oven to 375° and bake on ungreased cookie sheet for 10-12 minutes.

With gratitude to whoever paid for it.

VIRGINIA BELL'S GINGERBREAD

Makes 15 generous portions

4 cups whole wheat pastry flour
2 tbsp. baking soda
2 tsp. ground cinnamon
2 tsp. ground ginger
1 tsp. ground cloves
1 tsp. salt
3/4 cup honey
2 cups molasses
1 cup unsalted butter
3 large eggs
2 cups hot water

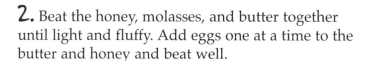

1. Sift all the dry ingredients together and set aside.

2. Beat the honey, molasses, and butter together until light and fluffy. Add eggs one at a time to the butter and honey and beat well.

3. In a large bowl combine wet and dry ingredients, moistening with hot water.

4. Grease and flour a 9"x13" baking pan. Bake at 350° for 30–40 minutes. Serve with fresh whipped cream.

> The gingerbread is very moist and the molasses gives it a chocolatey taste.

On November 2, 2003, my best friend Molly Sullivan died. The last time I saw Molly before she died, we spent the entire day planning all the dates she would return from the afterlife for a visit. What else would you do if you knew that was the last time you'd see your best friend? One of those special times we agreed upon was the fifteenth annual New Year's reunion with our other best friends, Mary Feeley and Corrine McGuigan, in Los Angeles. While there was no doubt in my mind that Molly would join us for the reunion, I don't think the others were expecting to see her so clearly.

It was three months after Molly died, and while we were very conscious of Molly's playful spirit from the time we met, it wasn't until the third day, when we went to the Santa Anita racetrack, that Molly made her presence delightfully clear. In search of some obvious sign of Molly with us, we bought the racing form and looked through all the Santa Anita races that afternoon for a horse named "Molly" or "Sullivan" or something similar. No horse came even remotely close to either name.

At that point I felt that we were being played with by Molly, and I was right. After the Santa Anita listings in the racing form the races for the Golden Gate Fields racetrack in San Francisco were listed. That's when we knew for sure that Molly was with us, because if her horse would be at any racetrack, it would of course be at the Golden Gate. Hardly able to contain our excitement, we went through race after race at Golden Gate Fields looking for Molly's horse. And then we saw it. In race number nine, the last race of the day, the horse slated to come in first was named "Sullivanitis." Words still can't describe what we felt at that moment. We placed our $20 bet on "Sullivanitis" and then rushed home to get the results on the computer.

In preparation for the big moment we made Molly's favorite artichoke dip ("Hot Artichoke Dip," page 18), and whipped up a pitcher of Manhattans ("Judy's Manhattans," page 17). Then we sat around the computer, eyes glued to the screen, awaiting the results. When "Sullivanitis" came in last we looked at each other with surprise and saw that Molly was with us as clear as she could be. At the "Golden Gate," where Molly is, of course, "The first will be last and the last will come in first."

To this day we still laugh over Molly joining us at the racetrack. Not only that, but weeks later, in telling the story to friends, we learned that Seabiscuit was the last movie Molly saw before she died, and Seabiscuit the horse performed his miracle at the Santa Anita racetrack the year Molly was born, 1938. Needless to say, every year we three look forward to Molly joining us for our annual reunion.

Fun is a sacrament in my life and an essential ingredient in every meal. The laughter and food shared with loved ones always lifts my spirits in a way that nothing else can. The magic ingredient that makes fun and food a sacrament is you and those you gather around your table. The love you have for one another is what transforms a meal into a miracle.

My final hope in ending this book is that you too might be moved to do what I did here. Put together a book of your favorite recipes and funny stories. Add photos, illustrations, favorite quotes, and helpful hints. That's the sacred stuff that helps change daily bread into the daily miracles that feed our bodies, our souls, and our funnybones. There is no greater gift than that kind of book. May your life be full of such delicious and fun-filled miracles. Blessed be.

INDEX

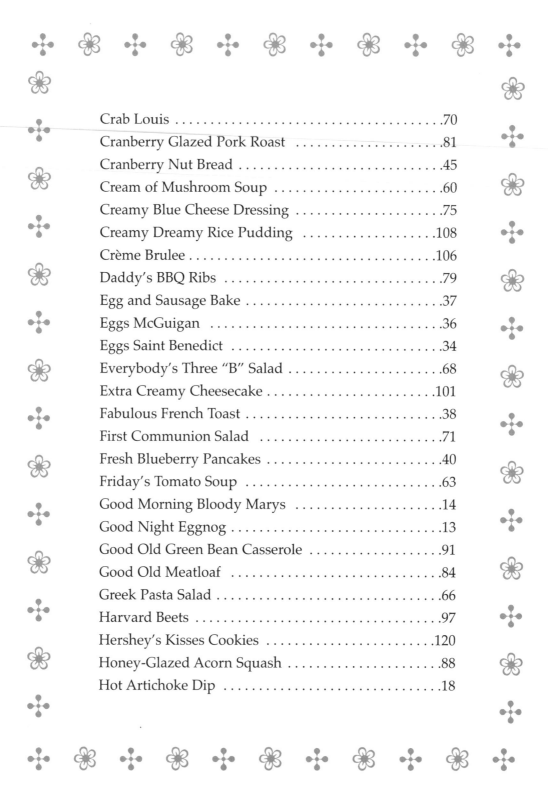